HEALTH CARE IN TRANSITION

AF764592

PRIVATE HEALTH INSURANCE AND ESSENTIAL HEALTH BENEFITS

PREMIUM AND COVERAGE VARIATIONS

HEALTH CARE IN TRANSITION

Additional books in this series can be found on Nova's website under the Series tab.

Additional e-books in this series can be found on Nova's website under the e-book tab.

HEALTH CARE IN TRANSITION

PRIVATE HEALTH INSURANCE AND ESSENTIAL HEALTH BENEFITS

PREMIUM AND COVERAGE VARIATIONS

CHERYL BENNETT
EDITOR

NOVINKA
New York

Library of Congress Cataloging-in-Publication Data

ISBN: 978-1-63484-819-0

Published by Nova Science Publishers, Inc. † New York

CONTENTS

PREFACE

The Patient Protection and Affordable Care Act (PPACA), as of 2014, changed how insurers determine health insurance premiums and how consumers shop for individual market health insurance plans. For example, PPACA prohibited insurers from denying coverage or varying premiums based on consumer health status or gender. At the same time, PPACA required health plans to be marketed based on their metal tiers (bronze, silver, gold, and platinum), which helps consumers compare the relative value of each plan; it also required the establishment of health insurance exchanges in each state, through which consumers can compare and select from among participating health plans. This book examines the numbers of health plans available to individuals and how they changed from 2014 to 2015; and the range of health insurance premiums in 2014 and 2015, and how they changed for individuals in each state and county for selected consumers. The book discusses premium and coverage variations of private health insurance and essential health benefits.

In: Private Health Insurance and Essential Health… ISBN: 978-1-63484-819-0
Editor: Cheryl Bennett

Chapter 1

PRIVATE HEALTH INSURANCE: THE RANGE OF PREMIUMS AND PLAN AVAILABILITY FOR INDIVIDUALS IN 2014 AND 2015*

United States Government Accountability Office

ABBRAVIATION

AV	actuarial value
CCIIO	Center for Consumer Information and Insurance Oversight
CMS	Centers for Medicare & Medicaid Services
FFE	federally facilitated exchange
PPACA	Patient Protection and Affordable Care Act
SBE	state-based exchange

WHY GAO DID THIS STUDY

PPACA, as of 2014, changed how insurers determine health insurance premiums and how consumers shop for individual market health insurance plans. For example, PPACA prohibited insurers from denying coverage or varying premiums based on consumer health status or gender. At the same

* This is an edited, reformatted and augmented version of The United States Government Accountability Office publication, GAO-15-687, dated August 2015.

time, PPACA required health plans to be marketed based on their metal tiers (bronze, silver, gold, and platinum), which helps consumers compare the relative value of each plan; it also required the establishment of health insurance exchanges in each state, through which consumers can compare and select from among participating health plans.

GAO was asked to examine variation in the health plan options and premiums available to individuals under PPACA, and how the options available in 2014 compared to those in 2015. GAO examined: (1) the numbers of health plans available to individuals and how they changed from 2014 to 2015, and (2) the range of health insurance premiums in 2014 and 2015, and how they changed for individuals in each state and county for selected consumers. GAO analyzed data from the Centers for Medicare & Medicaid Services (CMS); reviewed applicable statutes, regulations, guidance, and other documentation; and interviewed officials from CMS. Comparisons across years were conducted for states that had sufficiently reliable data in both years—including comparisons of plans offered either on or off an exchange in 28 states (1,886 counties) and comparisons of plans offered only on an exchange for 38 states (2,613 counties) although GAO is reporting some data on 49 states.

WHY GAO DID THIS STUDY

The Patient Protection and Affordable Care Act (PPACA), as of 2014, changed how insurers determine health insurance premiums and how consumers shop for individual market health insurance plans. For example, PPACA prohibited insurers from denying coverage or varying premiums based on consumer health status or gender. At the same time, PPACA required health plans to be marketed based on their metal tiers (bronze, silver, gold, and platinum), which helps consumers compare the relative value of each plan; it also required the establishment of health insurance exchanges in each state, through which consumers can compare and select from among participating health plans.

GAO was asked to examine variation in the health plan options and premiums available to individuals under PPACA, and how the options available in 2014 compared to those in 2015. GAO examined: (1) the numbers of health plans available to individuals and how they changed from 2014 to 2015, and (2) the range of health insurance premiums in 2014 and 2015, and how they changed for individuals in each state and county for selected consumers. GAO analyzed data from the Centers for Medicare & Medicaid Services (CMS); reviewed applicable statutes, regulations, guidance, and other documentation; and interviewed officials from CMS. Comparisons across years were conducted for states that had sufficiently reliable data in both years—including comparisons of plans offered either on or off an exchange in 28 states (1,886 counties) and comparisons of plans offered only on an exchange for 38 states (2,613 counties) although GAO is reporting some data on 49 states.

WHAT GAO FOUND

As of 2014, key provisions of the Patient Protection and Affordable Care Act (PPACA) resulted in the establishment of health insurance exchanges in each state and changed how insurers determined health insurance premiums. Individual market consumers generally had access to more health plans in 2015 compared to 2014, and in both years the lowest-cost plans were available through exchanges in most of the 1,886 counties GAO analyzed in the 28 states for which it had sufficiently reliable data for plans offered either on or off an exchange. In addition, consumers in most of the counties analyzed had six or more plans to choose from in three of the four health plan metal tiers (bronze, silver, and gold) in both 2014 and 2015, and the percentage of counties with six or more plans in those metal tiers increased from 2014 to 2015. Consumers had fewer options regarding platinum plans, although the availability of platinum plans generally also increased from 2014 to 2015. The lowest-cost plan available in a county was available on an exchange in most counties. For example, among the 1,886 counties analyzed, GAO found that the lowest-cost silver plan for a 30-year-old was available on an exchange in 63 percent of these counties in 2014 and in 81 percent of these counties in 2015—an increase of 18 percentage points.

The range of premiums available to consumers in 2014 and 2015 varied among the states and counties GAO analyzed. For example, in Arizona the lowest-cost silver plan option for a 30-year-old was $147 per month in both years, but in Maine, the lowest-cost silver plan options for a 30-year-old were $252 in 2014 and $237 in 2015. In the 28 states included in GAO's analysis, from 2014 to 2015 the minimum premiums for silver plans available to a 30-year-old increased in 18 states, decreased in 9 states, and remained unchanged in 1 state. At the county level, GAO found that premiums for the lowest-cost silver option available for a 30-year-old increased by 5 percent or more in 51 percent of the counties in the 28 states. GAO also found that the range of premiums—from the lowest to highest cost—differed considerably by state. For example, in Rhode Island, 2014 premiums for silver plans available to a 30-year-old either on or off an exchange ranged from a low of $241 per month to a high of $266 per month, a difference of 10 percent, and in 2015 ranged from a low of $217 per month to a high of $285 per month, a difference of 32 percent. By contrast, in Arizona, 2014 premiums for these plans ranged from a low of $147 per month to a high of $508 per month, a difference of 244 percent, and in 2015 ranged from a low of $147 per month to a high of $545 per month, a difference of 270 percent.

An interactive graphic reporting by state and county the minimum, median, and maximum premium values for all individual market plans (either on or off the exchange) and for exchange-only plans, is available at http://www.gao.gov/products/GAO-15-687. It includes either data for both years, or partial data (e.g., data for one of the two years) for 49 states.

GAO received technical comments on a draft of this report from the Department of Health and Human Services and incorporated them as appropriate.

* * *

August 10, 2015

The Honorable Orrin G. Hatch
Chairman
Committee on Finance United States Senate

The Honorable Fred Upton Chairman
Committee on Energy and Commerce
House of Representatives

Millions of Americans obtain health coverage by purchasing private health insurance plans in the individual market.[1] These Americans purchase health insurance for a variety of reasons, including being self-employed or a small business owner, or because their own employer does not offer insurance. The Patient Protection and Affordable Care Act (PPACA), as of 2014, changed how insurers determine health insurance premiums and how consumers shop for individual market health insurance plans.[2] For example, PPACA prohibited insurers from denying coverage to any individuals and from varying premiums based on consumer health status or gender. It also established limits on premium variation based on age, geographic location, and other factors.[3] In addition, PPACA established requirements for the benefits that must be covered by health plans—referred to as essential health benefits—and required insurers to market their plans according to defined categories comparing the extent to which the plans would be expected to cover the costs of enrollees' medical care.[4]

PPACA also required the establishment of health insurance exchanges in each state beginning in 2014[5]—marketplaces through which individual market consumers can compare and select health insurance coverage from among all the health plans participating in the exchange.[6] Some states have established their own exchanges—referred to as state-based exchanges (SBE). For consumers in states that have not done so, a federal exchange has been established—which we refer to as the Federally Facilitated Exchange (FFE). In general, plans available on either an SBE or the FFE are also available for sale outside of the exchange. The combination of all of these provisions allowed consumers to directly compare the individual market health insurance plans available to them based on premium costs, benefits covered, and plan generosity.

You asked us to examine the health plan options available to individual market consumers under this new paradigm, the extent to which plan options and premium costs available to consumers vary throughout the United States, and how the plan options available in 2014 compared to those in 2015. This report examines: (1) the numbers of health insurance plans available to individual market consumers and how they changed from 2014 to 2015, and (2) the range of health insurance premiums in 2014 and 2015 and how they changed for individual market consumers in each state and county for selected consumers.

For both of our objectives we reviewed applicable statutes, regulations, guidance, and other documentation, and we analyzed two sources of data maintained by the Centers for Medicare & Medicaid Services' (CMS), Center for Consumer Information and Insurance Oversight (CCIIO)—the FFE and Plan Finder databases—which included information on health plans offered to consumers in calendar years 2014 and 2015. The FFE database included data on all of the plans that were offered through the FFE. These data were publicly available to consumers shopping for FFE health plans using the Healthcare.gov website.[7] The Plan Finder database included information on plans offered outside an exchange, including those offered exclusively outside the exchanges as well as those available on or off the exchanges. These data were publicly available to consumers shopping for health plans through the Plan Finder online portal.[8] The premium amounts and supporting plan information in the FFE and Plan Finder data sources were self-reported by each insurer, and each insurer was required to comply with a data validation and attestation process.

Using these data, we analyzed aspects of plans offered to certain categories of consumers at the state and county level, whether or not the plans were offered on or off of an exchange. These included analyses of the numbers of plans and premium costs available to the consumers in each year and analyses of the changes in these numbers and costs between 2014 and 2015. We selected the consumer categories to represent the broad range of consumers who would shop for individual market insurance. They included nonsmoking: individuals, aged 19; individuals, aged 30; families of four, parents aged 40; couples aged 55; and individuals, aged 64. We also conducted analyses at the state and county level that focused on plans offered through an exchange for these same categories of consumers. Our analyses focused on two categories of plans—exchange plans (plans that were available on an exchange) and all plans (whether or not they were available on an exchange)—for both 2014 and 2015. Our analyses do not reflect the entire universe of insurers' premiums for plans sold on the SBEs or plans not sold through exchanges, because the data for plans sold on the SBEs or plans not sold through exchanges in the Plan Finder database were incomplete.[9] Because of this, we made certain exceptions in our reporting and only reported data for states for which we had sufficiently reliable data, as follows:

- For our analysis of the numbers of health insurance plans available to individual market consumers and how they changed from 2014 to 2015, we excluded from our analyses states where the percentage of plans that reported premium data was less than 70 percent of the universe of plans in either of the 2 years. We also excluded the state of Virginia from our analyses because the 2014 FFE data for that state included data that appeared to be erroneous. After these exclusions, our analyses of all plans included data from 28 of the 50 states and the 1,886 counties within those states, and our analysis that was limited to exchange plans included data for 38 of the 50 states and the 2,613 counties within those states.[10]
- For our analysis showing the range of health insurance premiums in 2014 and 2015 by county and year, we applied the same exclusions noted above for all comparisons of data across years.

- In an interactive graphic that reports the range of premiums by state and county, we reported all data that was deemed sufficiently reliable for each combination of plan category (exchange or all plans) and year. As a result, we reported data for 49 states, including: complete sets of data for 25 states for which we had sufficiently reliable data for both plan categories in both years; and partial sets of data for 24 states for which we had sufficiently reliable data only for certain elements. For example, in a state where we had information for fewer than 70 percent of exchange plans in a given year, the interactive graphic does not include any values for exchange plans for that state in that year. We did not include any data for one state (Washington) or for the District of Columbia because the data were not sufficiently reliable in either of the plan categories in either year. See Appendix I for details on the reliability of the data for each state.

To assess the reliability of the FFE data we interviewed CCIIO officials with knowledge of these data. Officials confirmed that because the data we obtained included all of the FFE health plan information that was publicly available to consumers shopping for FFE insurance plans using the Healthcare.gov website, those data effectively represented the full universe of FFE plans and premium values available to consumers in each year. To assess the reliability of the Plan Finder data, we reviewed the requirements for the data validation and attestation process; reviewed documentation on the database that houses the information submitted to CCIIO; and interviewed key CCIIO officials responsible for overseeing the submission and maintenance of the data. This allowed us to determine that the data were sufficiently reliable for our purposes.

We conducted this performance audit from August 2014 to August 2015 in accordance with generally accepted government auditing standards. Those standards require that we plan and perform the audit to obtain sufficient, appropriate evidence to provide a reasonable basis for our findings and conclusions based on our audit objectives. We believe that the evidence obtained provides a reasonable basis for our findings and conclusions based on our audit objectives.

BACKGROUND

Individual Market Insurance under PPACA

Beginning January 1, 2014, PPACA required that health insurance plans, whether sold on or off an exchange, offer a comprehensive package of items and services—known as essential health benefits. At the same time, PPACA required most individuals to maintain minimum essential coverage for themselves and their dependents or pay a tax penalty—this requirement is commonly referred to as the individual mandate.[11] Individuals who do not have other insurance coverage, such as from an employer, may satisfy this requirement by maintaining coverage under health plans offered in the individual market.

Certain PPACA provisions affected the way individual market plans are marketed for consumers. In particular, PPACA standardized health insurance plans into four "metal" tiers of coverage—bronze, silver, gold, and platinum—which reflect out-of-pocket costs that may be incurred by an enrollee. Bronze plans tend to have the lowest premiums but leave consumers subject to the highest out-of-pocket costs when they receive health care services, while platinum plans tend to have the highest premiums and the lowest out-of-pocket costs.[12]

- The generosity of each metal tier is measured by the plan's actuarial value (AV). AV is expressed as the percentage of covered medical expenses estimated to be paid by the insurer for a standard population and set of allowed charges for in-network providers.[13] The higher the AV percentage, the lower the expected enrollee cost sharing. For example, for a plan with an AV of 70 percent, it is expected that, on average, enrollee cost sharing under that plan will be 30 percent of the cost of care, while for a plan with an AV of 80 percent, it is expected that, on average, enrollee cost sharing under that plan will be 20 percent of the cost of care.
- PPACA includes standards related to AV and assigns a specific actuarial value to each of the four metal tiers: bronze (AV = 60 percent); silver (AV =70 percent); gold (AV = 80 percent); and platinum (AV = 90 percent). If an insurer sells a plan on an exchange, it must at least offer one plan at the silver level and one plan at the

gold level. Insurers are not required to offer bronze or platinum versions of their plans in order to participate on exchanges.

PPACA provisions also affected the way individual market plans are priced for consumers. For example, PPACA prohibited health insurers from varying health insurance plan premiums on the basis of factors other than age, geographic location and tobacco use—for which limits were established. For example, the age factor used to adjust premiums may vary by no more than a 3 to 1 ratio for adults aged 21 and older and must use a uniform age rating curve to specify the rates across all adult age bands. Premium variation based on health status or gender was effectively prohibited.

Incentives to Shop for Plans Offered through Exchanges

PPACA does not require insurers to offer plans through the state or federal exchanges. Similarly, it does not require consumers to purchase plans through the exchanges; however, there are incentives for many consumers to do so. For example, certain consumers earning from 100 to 400 percent of the federal poverty level are eligible to receive premium tax credits that can reduce premium costs, but only for plans purchased through an exchange.[14] Similarly, certain consumers earning from more than 100 percent to 250 percent of the federal poverty level are eligible to receive additional subsidies that help them pay for the out of pocket costs, but only for silver plans purchased through an exchange.[15] Also, the SBEs and FFE allow consumers to comparison shop for plans and enroll in a plan online, whether or not consumers are eligible for premium tax credits or cost sharing subsidies.

Individual Market Consumers Generally Had Access to More Plans in 2015 Compared to 2014, and the Lowest-Cost Plans Were Available through Exchanges in Most Counties in Both Years

Individual market consumers in every county in our analysis had access to a variety of plan options each year, and the number of plans available to consumers generally increased from 2014 to 2015. For example, in 28 states for which we had reliable data for all plans (offered either on or off exchanges), the percentage of counties for which six or more plan options were available to consumers increased from 2014 to 2015 for three of the metal tiers—bronze, silver, and gold—and in 2015 consumers in every county in these states had access to six or more plans in each of these three metal tiers.[16] Further, in 2015, among the 38 states where we focused our analysis on plans offered on an exchange, we found that consumers in 88 percent of the counties had access to six or more bronze exchange plans, consumers in 94 percent of counties had access to six or more silver exchange plans, and consumers in 71 percent of counties had access to six or more gold exchange plans. Not all consumers had access to platinum plans, however, the availability of platinum plans generally also increased from 2014 to 2015. (See table 1.)

Table 1. The Percentages of Counties in Which Various Numbers of Health Plans Were Offered to Individual Market Consumers, by Market Category and Metal Tier, 2014 and 2015

Market Category	Metal tier	Percentage of counties in 2014			Percentage of counties in 2015		
		No plans available	Between 1 and 5 plans available	6 or more plans available	No plans available	Between 1 and 5 plans available	6 or more plans available
All plans (available on or off exchange)[a]	Bronze	0%	3%	97%	0%	0%	100%
	Silver	0	3	97	0	0	100
	Gold	0	5	95	0	0	100
	Platinum	9	31	60	1	15	84
Plans available on an exchange[b]	Bronze	0	20	80	0	12	88
	Silver	0	20	80	0	6	94
	Gold	0	41	59	0	29	71
	Platinum	46	48	7	31	63	6

Source: GAO analysis of Center for Consumer Information and Insurance Oversight data. | GAO-15-687.

Note: Figures may not total 100 across rows within each year due to rounding.

[a]Includes data for plans in the 1,886 counties in the 28 states for which we had sufficiently reliable data on plans whether or not they were sold through an exchange.

[b]Includes data for plans in the 2,613 counties in the 38 states for which we had sufficiently reliable data on plans sold through exchanges.

We also found that the lowest-cost plan options available in a county were available on an exchange in a majority of the counties included in our analysis. For example, among the 1,886 counties in the 28 states for which we had sufficiently reliable data for plans both on and off an exchange, we found that the lowest-cost silver plan option for a 30-year old was available on an exchange in 63 percent of the counties in 2014 and in 81 percent of the counties in 2015—an increase of 18 percentage points.

THE RANGE OF PREMIUMS AVAILABLE TO CONSUMERS VARIED AMONG THE STATES AND COUNTIES IN OUR ANALYSIS IN BOTH 2014 AND 2015

Premiums Varied Widely among the States in Our Analysis, and from 2014 to 2015 Premiums Were More Likely to Increase than Decrease

The premiums for the lowest-cost plan options available in each state included in our analysis varied significantly from state to state. For example, in Arizona (a state for which the lowest-cost premiums were among the lowest in the country) the lowest-cost silver plan options for a 30-year-old were $147 per month in both years for plans both on and off an exchange. By contrast, in Maine (a state for which the lowest-cost premiums were among the highest in the country) the lowest-cost silver plan options for a 30-year-old were $252 in 2014 and $237 in 2015 for plans both on and off an exchange. Based on the full premium costs, on an annual basis in 2015 a 30-year-old in Arizona who was not eligible for a premium tax credit could have spent $1,082 less on the lowest-cost silver plan available to them compared to what the same consumer in Maine could have spent on the lowest-cost silver plan available to them.[17] The findings were similar when we conducted our analysis of plans offered on exchanges in 38 states. Because each state in our analysis uses a uniform age rating curve to specify the rates across all adult age bands, each state would have the same relative differences in premiums for all adult age categories. (See table 2.)

Table 2. Monthly Minimum and Median Premiums Available to a 30-Year-Old by State in 2014 and 2015, for Silver Tier Health Plans Available either on or off an Exchange

	Minimum premium value (in			Median premium value (in		
State	2014	2015	Difference	2014	2015	Difference
Alabama	$199	$215	$16	$227	$279	$52
Arkansas	188	233	45	278	278	0
Arizona	147	147	0	273	309	36
California	201	205	4	286	310	24
Colorado	213	173	(40)	343	369	26
Connecticut	245	206	(39)	305	307	2
Florida	181	195	14	279	315	36
Georgia	188	202	14	296	321	25
Hawaii	157	173	16	217	180	(37)
Iowa	171	173	2	262	290	28
Illinois	170	185	15	294	302	8
Indiana	215	175	(40)	310	339	29
Kansas	167	170	3	243	239	(4)
Kentucky	163	148	(15)	279	259	(20)
Louisiana	218	245	27	309	340	31
Maine	252	237	(15)	324	323	(1)
Massachusetts	222	192	(30)	364	361	(3)
Michigan	169	194	25	278	285	7
Mississippi	233	219	(14)	317	322	5
Nebraska	194	217	23	318	337	19
Ohio	192	206	14	287	313	26
Oklahoma	163	172	9	287	315	28
Pennsylvania	145	151	6	220	274	54
Rhode Island	241	217	(24)	261	255	(6)
South Dakota	224	226	2	377	279	(98)
Tennessee	160	161	1	243	269	26
Utah	162	186	24	253	251	(2)
Wisconsin	214	211	(3)	299	336	37

Source: GAO analysis of Center for Consumer Information and Insurance Oversight data. | GAO-15-687.

Note: Includes data for plans in 1,886 counties in the 28 states included in our analysis for which we had sufficiently reliable data on plans whether or not they were sold through an exchange.

[a]The premium amounts paid by individuals who received premium tax credits would have been offset and therefore effectively lower than the premium costs we

provide in this report. Similarly, cost sharing subsidies would reduce the out-of-pocket costs to the enrollee which would, in effect, make the actual benefit of the plans higher that what the actuarial values implied.

[b]The median plan value represents either 1) the plan with the median premium value in the category (when there was an odd number of plans within that category), or 2) the average of the premiums of the two plans that were closest to the median (when there was an even number of plans within the category).

The premiums for the median-cost plan options available in each state included in our analysis also varied widely. For example, in both years Hawaii had among the lowest median premium costs for silver plans offered to a 30-year-old either on or off the exchange—$217 per month in 2014 and $180 per month in 2015. By contrast, in both years Colorado had among the highest median premium costs for such plans—$343 per month in 2014 and $369 per month in 2015.

In most states, the costs for the minimum and median premiums for silver plans increased from 2014 to 2015. For example, in the 28 states included in our analysis, from 2014 to 2015 the minimum premium values for silver plans available to a 30-year-old increased in 18 states, decreased in 9 states, and remained unchanged in 1 state. Similarly, in these same states the median premium values for silver plans available to 30-year-old increased in 19 states, decreased in 8 states and remained unchanged in 1 state.

Further, in general, states with higher than average minimum premiums in 2014 were more likely to have declines in 2015 premiums than the states with lower than average minimum premiums in 2014. For example, the average minimum monthly premium value for the silver plan option for a 30-year-old in 2014 in the 28 states included in our analysis was $193 for plans offered on or off an exchange. Of the 13 states with 2014 premiums for this group of consumers that were greater than $193, eight had lower minimum premiums in 2015. Of the 15 states with 2014 premiums for this group of consumers that were less than $193, only one state had a lower minimum premium in 2015.

When analyzing premium costs at the county level, we found that from 2014 to 2015, premiums were more likely to increase than decrease. For example, our analysis of the minimum premiums for silver plans in states where we analyzed data on plans offered either on or off exchanges found that premiums for a 30-year-old increased by 5 percent or more in 51 percent of the counties. During the same time period, premiums for these plans decreased by 5 percent or more in nearly 17 percent of the counties, and increased or decreased by less than 5 percent in 32 percent of the counties. The findings were similar when we repeated this analysis using the median premium value in each county and when we limited the analysis to plans offered on exchanges. Because each state in our analysis uses a uniform age rating curve to specify the rates across all adult age bands, each state would have the same relative differences in premiums for all adult age categories. (See table 3.)

Table 3. The Percentages of Counties for Which the Minimum and Median Premiums for a Silver Health Plan for a 30-Year-Old Decreased, Held Steady, or Increased from 2014 to 2015

		Dec-reased		Held steady		Increased	
	10 per-cent or more	Between 5 and less than 10 percent	Between 1 and less than 5 percent	Change of less than 1 percent	Between 1 and less than 5 percent	Between 5 and less than 10 percent	10 percent or more
Minimum premium value,							
All plans (available on or off exchange)[a]	7.8%	9.1%	8.3%	8.7%	15.4%	29.4%	21.4%
Plans available on an exchange[b]	10.0	8.4	7.8	8.3	14.0	30.8	20.8
Median premium value							
All plans (available on or off exchange)[a]	6.6	7.1	11.1	6.3	16.1	22.0	30.9
Plans available on an exchange[b]	10.6	7.7	10.3	6.4	11.7	19.6	33.6

Source: GAO analysis of Center for Consumer Information and Insurance Oversight data. | GAO-15-687.

Note: Because each state in our analysis uses a uniform age rating curve to specify the rates across all adult age bands, these same findings would apply to premiums for all adult age categories.

[a]Includes data for plans available in the 1,886 counties in the 28 states included in our analysis for which we had sufficiently reliable data on plans whether or not they were sold through an exchange.

[b]Includes data for plans available in the 2,613 counties in the 38 states included in our analysis for which we had sufficiently reliable data on plans sold through exchanges.

The Ranges of Premiums Available to Consumers Were Much Narrower in Some States Compared to Others

We found that the range of premiums—from the lowest to highest cost—available to consumers differed considerably for the states included in our analysis. For example, our analysis of premiums for silver plans available to a 30-year-old either on or off an exchange found that the ranges of premiums available were much more narrow in Rhode Island compared to Arizona. In Rhode Island, 2014 premiums for plans ranged from a low of $241 per month to a high of $266 per month, a difference of 10 percent, and in 2015 ranged from a low of $217 per month to a high of $285 per month, a difference of 32 percent. By contrast, in Arizona, 2014 premiums for these plans ranged from a low of $147 per month to a high of $508 per month, a difference of 244 percent, and in 2015 ranged from a low of $147 per month to a high of $545 per month, a difference of 270 percent. In addition, between 2014 and 2015, the range from the lowest- to highest-cost premiums available by state became wider in 18 out of the 28 states included in this analysis. The findings were similar when we conducted our analysis for plans offered on exchanges in 38 states.

We also found that the percentage difference between the minimum and maximum premium in the states included in our analysis was generally higher in states where the average number of plans available per county was higher. For example, in both years, states with an average of 30 or more plans per county had among the widest ranges between the lowest and highest premium amounts. By contrast, states with an average of 15 or fewer plans per county had among the narrowest ranges between the lowest and highest premium amounts. (See table 4.) Because each state in our analysis uses a uniform age rating curve to specify the rates across all adult age bands, each state would have the same relative differences in premiums for all adult age categories.

When analyzing ranges at the county level, we found that among all the counties in our analysis, the range of premiums available for different plan options generally widened from 2014 to 2015. For example, among the 1,886 counties in the 28 states for which we had sufficiently reliable data on all plans offered on or off an exchange, we found that the range in silver plan premiums for a 30-year-old in 2015 was wider in 79 percent of the counties compared to 2014. The findings were similar when we conducted our analysis for plans offered on exchanges in 38 states.

Table 4. The Range of Premiums Available to a 30-Year-Old by State in 2014 and 2015, for Silver Tier Health Plans Available either on or off an Exchange

		2014				2015		
		Monthly premiums (dollars)[a]				Monthly premiums (dollars)[a]		
State	Average number of plans per county	Minimum premium value	Maximum premium value	Percent differ-rence	Average number of plans per county	Minimum premium value	Maximum premium value	Percent differ-rence
Alabama	5	$199	$332	67%	22	$215	$425	98%
Arkansas	31	188	386	105	31	233	369	59
State	Average number of plans per county	Minimum premium value	Maximum premium value	Percent differ-rence	Average number of plans per county	Minimum premium value	Maximum premium value	Percent differ-rence
Arizona	35	147	508	244	42	147	545	270
California	19	201	427	112	18	205	492	141
Colorado	39	213	592	178	40	173	680	294
Connecticut	21	245	391	60	38	206	410	99
Florida	29	181	428	137	42	195	503	158
Georgia	38	188	444	136	48	202	525	160
Hawaii	10	157	223	42	11	173	196	14
Iowa	36	171	383	125	37	173	377	118
Illinois	39	170	434	155	45	185	558	201
Indiana	15	215	372	73	40	175	548	213
Kansas	36	167	356	114	32	170	362	112
Kentucky	20	163	387	137	14	148	343	131
Louisiana	27	218	418	92	32	245	446	82
Maine	8	252	400	59	19	237	475	100
Massachusetts	102	222	522	135	196	192	534	179
Michigan	18	169	428	153	40	194	407	110
Mississippi	25	233	422	81	24	219	507	131
Nebraska	18	194	346	79	25	217	396	82
Ohio	25	192	408	112	47	206	532	158
Oklahoma	26	163	358	119	27	172	437	154
Pennsylvania	22	145	403	178	32	151	412	172

		2014				2015		
		Monthly premiums (dollars)[a]				Monthly premiums (dollars)[a]		
State	Average number of plans per county	Minimum premium value	Maxi-mum premium value	Percent differ-rence	Average number of plans per county	Mini-mum premium value	Maxi-mum premium value	Percent differ-rence
Rhode Island	7	241	266	10	10	217	285	32
South Dakota	36	224	504	125	33	226	505	124
Tennessee	62	160	393	146	73	161	413	156
Utah	38	162	389	140	65	186	419	125
Wisconsin	67	214	490	129	67	211	533	152

Source: GAO analysis of Center for Consumer Information and Insurance Oversight data. | GAO-15-687.

Note: Includes plans available in the 28 states included in our analysis for which we had sufficiently reliable data on plans whether or not they were sold through an exchange. Because each state in our analysis uses a uniform age rating curve to specify the rates across all adult age bands, these same relative differences in premiums would apply to premiums for all adult age categories.

[a]The premium amounts paid by individuals who received premium tax credits would have been offset and therefore effectively lower than the premium costs we report. Similarly, cost sharing subsidies would reduce the out-of-pocket costs to the enrollee, which would, in effect, make the actual benefit of the plan higher that what the actuarial values implied.

In the interactive graphic linked to below, we provide files showing the range of health insurance premiums, by county, that were available to selected categories of consumers for exchange plans and all plans (whether or not they were available on an exchange)—for both 2014 and 2015. Twenty-five states include complete sets of data for both years. Twenty-four states include partial data if certain date elements were not sufficiently reliable to report. For example, in a state where we had information for fewer than 70 percent of exchange plans in a given year, we do not report any values for exchange plans for that state in that year. We do not include any data for the state of Washington or the District of Columbia because the data were either not available or not sufficient in both years. See figure 1 for an illustration of premium information available via the interactive map available at the website.

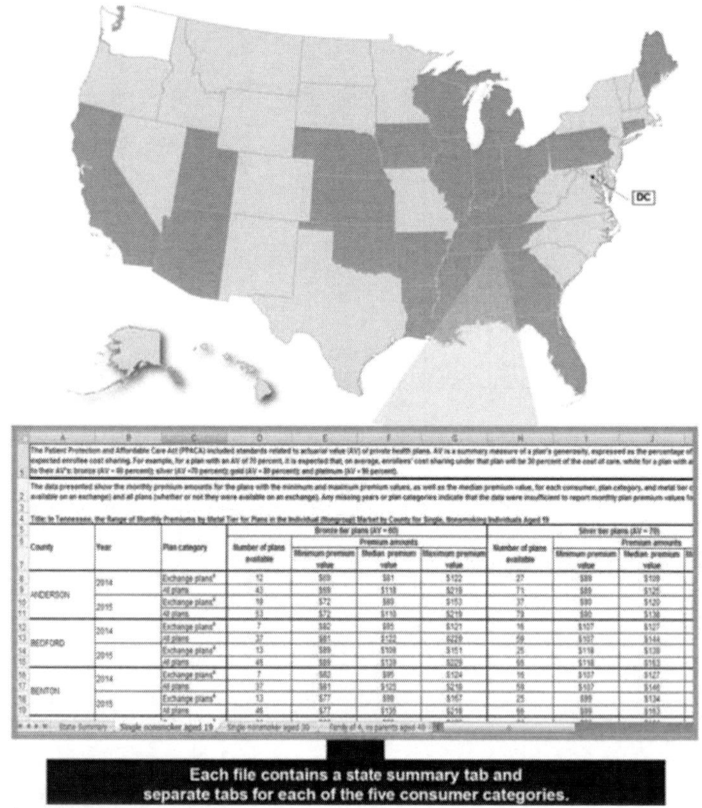

Surce: GAO (data) Map Resources (map). | GAO-15-687.

Figure 1. Illustration of Premium Interactive Map.

AGENCY COMMENTS

We received technical comments on a draft of this report from the Department of Health and Human Services and incorporated them as appropriate.

John E. Dicken
Director, Health Care

APPENDIX I: STATES INCLUDED AND EXCLUDED FROM GAO'S ANALYSES

State	Market type: federally facilitated exchange (FFE) or state based exchange (SBE)	Percent of plans offered on an exchange for which we have data		State included in analyses limited to plans available on an exchange(Y or N)	Percent of all plans for which we have data		
		2014	2015		2014	2015	(Y or N)
Alaska	FFE	100 %	100 %	Y	53%	96%	N
Alabama	FFE	100	100	Y	81	99	Y
Arkansas	FFE	100	100	Y	96	100	Y
Arizona	FFE	100	100	Y	82	95	Y
California	SBE	71	93	Y	83	91	Y
Colorado	SBE	82	61	N	87	80	Y
Connecticut	SBE	71	74	Y	71	78	Y
Delaware	FFE	100	100	Y	36	86	N
District of Columbia[a]	SBE	0	0	N	0	0	N
Florida	FFE	100	100	Y	78	90	Y
Georgia	FFE	100	100	Y	98	89	Y
Hawaii	SBE	61	100	N	72	100	Y
Iowa	FFE	100	100	Y	97	100	Y
Idaho	SBE	72	76	Y	61	86	N

Appendix I. (Continued)

State	Market type: federally facilitated exchange (FFE) or state based exchange (SBE)	Percent of plans offered on an exchange for which we have data		State included in analyses limited to plans available on an exchange(Y or N)	Percent of all plans for which we have data		
		2014	2015		2014	2015	(Y or N)
Illinois	FFE	100	100	Y	99	98	Y
Indiana	FFE	100	100	Y	72	90	Y
Kansas	FFE	100	100	Y	96	93	Y
Kentucky	SBE	80	95	Y	72	97	Y
Louisiana	FFE	100	100	Y	88	91	Y
Massachusetts	SBE	45	72	N	71	79	Y
Maryland	SBE	17	67	N	22	83	N
Maine	FFE	100	100	Y	100	99	Y
Michigan	FFE	100	100	Y	88	99	Y
Minnesota	SBE	61	89	N	32	34	N
Missouri	FFE	100	100	Y	45	100	N
Mississippi	FFE	100	100	Y	74	79	Y
Montana	FFE	100	100	Y	50	100	N
North Carolina	FFE	100	100	Y	57	72	N
North Dakota	FFE	100	100	Y	69	100	N
Nebraska	FFE	100	100	Y	97	100	Y
New Hampshire	FFE	100	100	Y	45	100	N
New Jersey	FFE	100	100	Y	61	88	N
New Mexico	SBE	27	90	N	51	83	N
Nevada	SBE	22	100	N	36	65	N
New York	SBE	40	74	N	52	79	N
Ohio	FFE	100	100	Y	79	93	Y
Oklahoma	FFE	100	100	Y	85	93	Y
Oregon	SBE	58	98	N	44	99	N

State	Market type: federally facilitated exchange (FFE) or state based exchange (SBE)	Percent of plans offered on an exchange for which we have data		State included in analyses limited to plans available on an exchange(Y or N)	Percent of all plans for which we have data		
		2014	2015		2014	2015	(Y or N)
Pennsyl-vania	FFE	100	100	Y	95	90	Y
Rhode Island	SBE	100	90	Y	100	94	Y
South Carolina	FFE	100	100	Y	46	89	N
South Dakota	FFE	100	100	Y	81	100	Y
Tennessee	FFE	100	100	Y	96	100	Y
Texas	FFE	100	100	Y	41	96	N
Utah	FFE	100	100	Y	86	88	Y
Virginia[b]	FFE	100	100	N	84	91	N
Vermont	SBE	45	100	N	22	100	N
Washing-ton	SBE	17	42	N	44	60	N
Wisconsin	FFE	100	100	Y	80	95	Y
West Virginia	FFE	100	100	Y	53	98	N
Wyoming	FFE	100	100	Y	22	100	N

Source: GAO analysis of Center for Consumer Information and Insurance Oversight data. | GAO-15-687.

[a] CCIIO did not provide individual market data for the District of Columbia.

[b] We excluded 2014 data for Virginia from our analyses because, even though the percentage of plans that reported premiums data was greater than 70 percent of the universe of plans in 2014, there were several outliers that made the data unreliable for this year.

End Notes

[1] Private health insurance includes individual and group market plans. Participants in the individual market purchase health insurance coverage directly from an insurer. Group market participants generally obtain health insurance coverage through a group health plan, usually offered by an employer.

[2] See the Patient Protection and Affordable Care Act (PPACA), Pub. L. No. 111-148, 124 Stat. 119 (2010), as amended by the Health Care and Education Reconciliation Act of 2010, (HCERA) Pub. L. No. 111-152,124 Stat.1029. In this report, references to PPACA include any amendments made by HCERA.

[3] See Pub. L. No. 111-148, §§ 1201(2), (4), 1562(c)(1), 10107(b)(1), 10103(a), 10107(b)(1), 124 Stat. 154,155, 264, 892, 911 (codified as amended at 42 U.S.C. §§ 300gg, 300gg-3). PPACA also included an individual mandate that requires most individuals to have health insurance coverage or pay a tax penalty. See Pub. L. No. 111- 148, §§ 1501, 10106, 124 Stat. 242, 907, as amended by, Pub. L. No. 111-152, §§ 1002, 1004, 124 Stat. 1032, 1034 (codified as amended at 26 U.S.C. § 5000A).

[4] We refer to the expected impact of the design of plan coverage on enrollee cost sharing as a plan's "generosity." A plan whose enrollees would incur lower out-of-pocket costs is more generous than one whose enrollees would incur higher costs.

[5] Some states use the term "marketplace" to refer to an insurance exchange.

[6] Pub. L. No. 111-148, §§ 1311(b), 1321(c), 124 Stat. 173, 186 (codified at 42 U.S.C. §§ 18031(b), 1841(c). Individuals can apply for plans sold through the exchanges either online, by phone, or with a paper application.

[7] see https://www.healthcare.gov/get-coverage/

[8] See https://finder.healthcare.gov/

[9] In addition, our analyses may include plans with little or no enrollment because enrollment data were not available.

[10] The analysis that was limited to plans offered through the exchanges included data from 33 of the 34 states that used the FFE, and data for 5 of 16 states that used SBEs.

[11] Individuals whose incomes are below statutory thresholds are exempt from the penalty

[12] In addition to these metal tiers, catastrophic plans are available to those under 30 years of age or to those who are exempt from the requirement to have minimum essential coverage because of a hardship or because the lowest-cost plan available would cost more than 8 percent of their household income. Catastrophic plans' actuarial value must be lower than that of a bronze plan.

[13] Health plans typically establish a network of providers with which they negotiate reimbursement rates. The actuarial value for each plan is calculated assuming all services are obtained within the network. Consumers who choose to access services from providers outside of their plans' networks may incur higher cost sharing.

[14] Premium tax credits will generally be available to eligible tax filers and their dependents who are (1) enrolled in one or more qualified health plans through an exchange, and (2) not eligible for other health insurance coverage. More specifically, to qualify for the premium tax credit, an individual or family must generally have income from 100 to 400 percent of the federal poverty level and not qualify for other health care coverage, such as Medicare, Medicaid, or employer-sponsored coverage that meets a minimum value standard specified in PPACA. The premium tax credit is calculated based on the second lowest-cost silver plan available to the consumer. Also, see GAO, Private Health Insurance: Early Evidence Finds Premium Tax Credit Likely Contributed to Expanded Coverage, but Some Lack Access to

Affordable Plans, GAO-15-312 (Washington, D.C.: March 23, 2013). We reported that, among those enrolling in federally facilitated exchanges during the 2014 open enrollment period, most (85 percent) were deemed eligible for the advance premium tax credit and that, on average, the premium tax credit reduced premiums by 76 percent.

[15] People who are eligible to receive a premium tax credit and have household incomes from 100 percent to 250 percent of poverty are also eligible for cost-sharing subsidies.

[16] If an insurer sells a plan on an exchange, it must at least offer one plan at the silver level and one plan at the gold level. Insurers are not required to offer bronze or platinum versions of their plans in order to participate on exchanges.

[17] In either state, the premium amount paid by individuals receiving the premium tax credit would be limited to a percentage of their income. As a result, individuals in Arizona and Maine with the same income would pay the same amount in premiums for the second-lowest-cost silver plan in 2015.

In: Private Health Insurance and Essential Health... ISBN: 978-1-63484-819-0
Editor: Cheryl Bennett

Chapter 2

THE PATIENT PROTECTION AND AFFORDABLE CARE ACT'S ESSENTIAL HEALTH BENEFITS (EHB)*

Namrata K. Uberoi

SUMMARY

The Patient Protection and Affordable Care Act (ACA; P.L. 111-148, as amended) requires all non-grandfathered health plans in the non-group and small-group private health insurance markets to offer a core package of health care services, known as the essential health benefits (EBB). The ACA does not specifically define this core package but rather lists 10 benefit categories from which benefits and services must be included.

The 10 benefit categories are as follows:

- ambulatory patient services;
- emergency services;
- hospitalization;
- maternity and newborn care;

* This is an edited, reformatted and augmented version of a Congressional Research Service publication R44163, prepared for Members and Committees of Congress, dated August 27, 2015.

- mental health and substance use disorder services, including behavioral health treatment;
- prescription drugs;
- rehabilitative and habilitative services and devices;
- laboratory services;
- preventive and wellness and chronic disease management; and
- pediatric services, including oral and vision care.

For 2014-2016, each state was required to select an EBB-benchmark plan. The benchmark plan serves as a reference plan on which non-group and small-group market plans must substantially base their benefits packages.

Because each state selected its own EBB-benchmark plan under the 2014-2016 approach to the EBB, there is considerable variation in EBB coverage from state to state. This variation occurs in terms of specific covered services as well as in terms of amount, duration, and scope. For example, some state EBB-benchmark plans may include bariatric surgery as a covered service whereas other state EBB-benchmark plans may not cover bariatric surgery. State benefit mandates also may be considered to be part of that state's EBB and thus add to state-level coverage differences.

Furthermore, because states can allow non-group and small-group plans to substitute certain services within the categories, coverage in plans within a state also may vary by benefit amount, duration, and scope. For example, a state's EBB-benchmark plan could offer up to 20 physical therapy visits and 10 occupational therapy visits. Another plan in the state could offer coverage consistent with the EBB-benchmark plan by covering up to 10 physical therapy visits and 20 occupational therapy visits.

In addition to covering the EBB, the ACA imposes a limit on cost sharing (which includes co-payments, coinsurance, and deductibles) for the EBB. The ACA also prohibits plans from applying lifetime and annual dollar limits on the EBB.

The Patient Protection and Affordable Care Act (ACA; P.L. 111-148, as amended) includes many provisions that apply to health plans offered in the private health insurance market. The private market often is described as having three segments: the non-group,[1] small-group, and large-group markets;[2] and many of the ACA's provisions focus specifically on the non-group and small-group insurance markets. These reforms are intended to address perceived failures in those markets, such as limited access to coverage and higher costs of coverage relative to the large-group market plans, and to provide some parity with the large-group market.[3] For example, benefit coverage in non-group and small-group market health plans generally was perceived to be limited in comparison to benefit coverage in large-group market health plans. Thus, to provide some similarity to plans in the large-group market, the ACA requires non-group and small-group health plans to offer the essential health benefits (EHB), which is a core package of health care services.

The EHB are one of the three components of the EHB package. The EHB package requires plans to (1) cover certain benefits (i.e., the essential health benefits); (2) comply with specific cost-sharing limitations; and (3) meet a certain generosity level.[4]

This report provides an overview of the first component of the EHB package—the essential health benefits. The report examines how the EHB are defined, regulations related to the EHB, state variation in the EHB, applicability of the EHB to health plans, and how the EHB interact with other ACA provisions.

Essential Health Benefits

Since 2014, all non-grandfathered[5] plans in the non-group and small-group[6] markets are required to offer a core package of health care services, known as the EHB. The ACA does not specifically define this core package. Instead, it lists 10 benefit categories from which benefits and services must be included (see *Figure 1*) and requires the Secretary of the Department of Health and Human Services (HHS) to further define the EHB.[7]

The HHS Secretary has the purview to define and periodically update the EHB. However, in defining the EHB, the HHS Secretary must take a number of parameters into account.[8] For example, the scope of the EHB is to be equivalent to the scope of benefits typically provided under an employer-sponsored insurance plan. To accomplish this task, the ACA requires the Secretary of the Department of Labor (DOL) to conduct surveys of employer-sponsored insurance plans to determine typical benefits and provide a summary of the findings to the HHS Secretary.

The EHB are to be balanced among the 10 categories, without a weighted preference toward any category. The HHS Secretary cannot make any coverage decisions, determine reimbursement rates, establish incentive programs, or design benefits in ways that discriminate against individuals because of their age, disability, or expected length of life. Furthermore, the

HHS Secretary must take into account the diverse health care needs of the population, which includes women, children, persons with disabilities, and other groups.

ESSENTIAL HEALTH BENEFITS

- Ambulatory patient services
- Emergency services
- Hospitalization
- Maternity and newborn care
- Mental health and substance use disorder services, including behavioral health treatment
- Prescription drugs
- Rehabilitative and habilitative services and devices
- Laboratory services
- Preventive and wellness services and chronic disease management
- Pediatric services, including oral and vision care

Source: 42 U.S.C. §18022.

Figure 1. The 10 Essential Health Benefits Categories.

The HHS Secretary is tasked with reviewing the EHB, and part of the EHB review process includes providing a report to Congress and the public. The report is supposed to assess whether enrollees are facing any difficulty accessing services, either due to coverage or cost, and to consider whether the EHB need to be modified or updated due to changes in medical evidence or scientific advancement. If any modifications are to be made, the HHS Secretary is to include in the report how the EHB would be modified. Consequently, the Secretary periodically may update the EHB based on issues identified during the review process.[9]

ESSENTIAL HEALTH BENEFITS FOR 2014-2016

State Selection of Benchmark Plans

In December 2011, the Centers for Medicare & Medicaid Services (CMS) released a bulletin that outlined a reference plan approach for the EHB.[10] This approach was based on employer-sponsored coverage in the current market. To define the EHB, HHS considered findings from the DOL's report[11] that described the scope of benefits under a typical employer-sponsored plan. HHS also considered a report[12] from the Institute of Medicine that recommended criteria and methods for determining and updating the EHB.

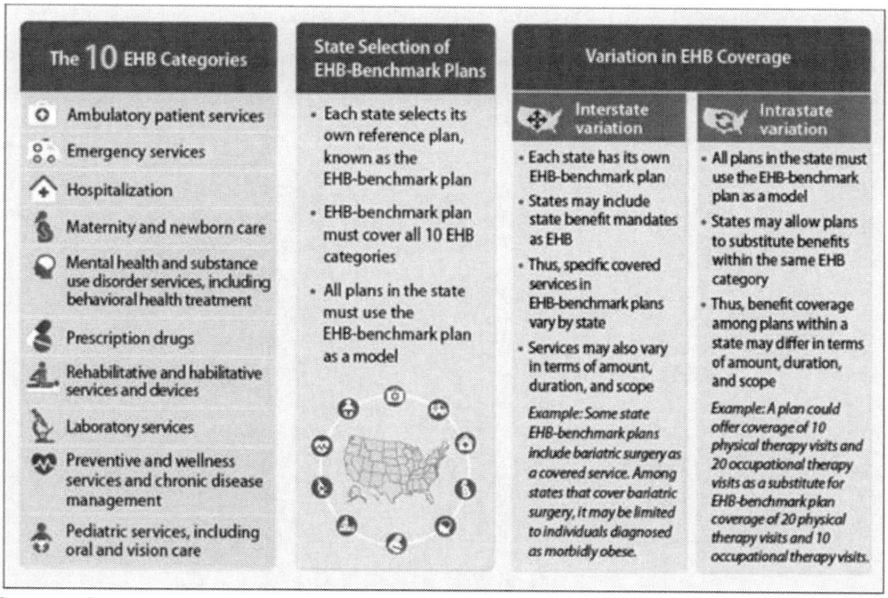

Source: Congressional Research Service (CRS) analysis of the essential health benefits (EHB) process based on 45 C.F.R. §156.100-115.

Figure 2. Overview of the Essential Health Benefits (EHB) Process.

The HHS Secretary outlined a process in which each state identified a single plan to serve as a reference plan on which most non-group and small-group market plans must base their benefits packages in terms of the scope of benefits offered (see *Figure 2*).[13] These reference plans are known as *EHB-benchmark plans.* The benchmark selection approach identified by the Secretary applied for the 2014, 2015,[14] and 2016[15] coverage years. Each state's EHB-benchmark plan applied to non-grandfathered health plans offered in the non-group and small-group[16] markets, both inside and outside the exchanges[17] (also known as *marketplaces*).

The process required each state[18] to select an EHB-benchmark plan that was based on plans available in the 2012 coverage year. States could select a benchmark plan among the following four options:

1) *Small-group market health plan.* Any of the three largest small-group market health plans, by enrollment, in that state;[19]
2) *State employee health benefit plan.* Any of the three largest employee health benefit plan options, by enrollment, available to state employees in that state;
3) *Federal Employees Health Benefits (FEHB) plan.* Any of the three largest national FEHB plan options, by aggregate enrollment;[20] or
4) *Non-Medicaid Health Maintenance Organization (HMO).* The largest insured commercial non-Medicaid HMO, by enrollment, operating in that state.

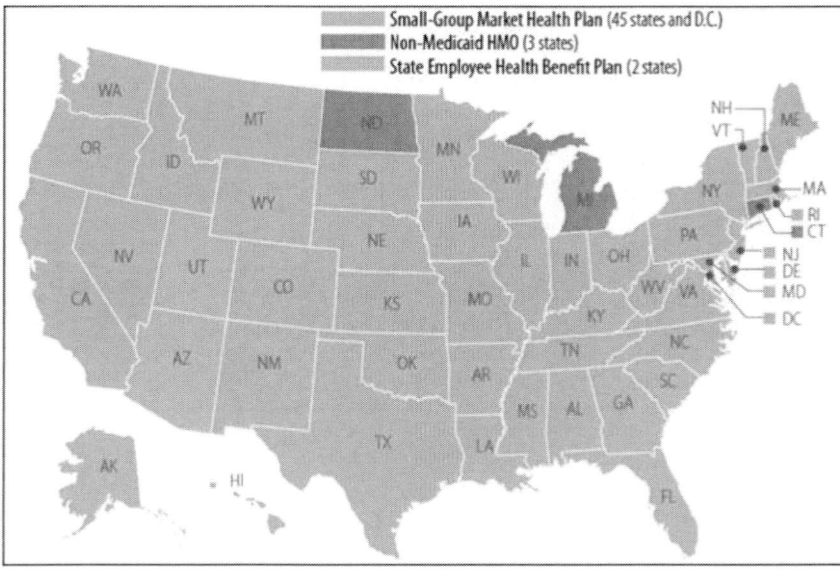

Source: CRS analysis of EHB-benchmark plan selection information from the Department of Health and Human Services, "Patient Protection and Affordable Care Act: Standards Related to Essential Health Benefits, Actuarial Value, and Accreditation," 78 Federal Register 12834-12872, February 25, 2013.

Notes: No state selected a Federal Employees Health Benefits (FEHB) plan as its essential health benefits benchmark plan for 2014-2016. HMO = health maintenance organization.

Figure 3. State Selection of 2014-2016 Essential Health Benefits Benchmark Plans.

If a state did not make a selection, the default EHB-benchmark plan was the largest health plan, by enrollment, in that state's small-group market.[21]

Each state's benchmark plan was finalized in early 2013. *Figure 3* maps the type of benchmark plan selected by each state. The EHB-benchmark plan for 45 states and the District of Columbia (DC) is the small-group market health plan. Three states selected a non-Medicaid HMO, and two states selected a state employee health benefit plan as their EHB-benchmark plans. No state selected an FEHB plan as its benchmark plan.[22]

Coverage in Each Benefit Category

According to the regulations, the EHB-benchmark plan had to provide coverage for all 10 EHB categories. However, a number of state benchmark plans did not include all 10 EHB categories. If the selected benchmark plan did not include items or services within a category, the plan had to be supplemented accordingly.[23]

Generally, if an EHB-benchmark plan did not cover 1 or more of the 10 EHB categories, the state supplemented the EHB-benchmark plan by adding that particular category in its entirety from another benchmark plan option (i.e., the small-group market health plan, state employee health benefit plan, FEHB plan, or non-Medicaid HMO options described in "State Selection of Benchmark Plans," above).

For states that did not select an EHB-benchmark plan and thus defaulted to an EHB-benchmark plan (the largest health plan, by enrollment, in that state's small-group market), HHS, if necessary, supplemented the state's EHB-benchmark plan. The default benchmark plan was supplemented in the following order: (1) the second-largest plan, by enrollment, in the state's small-group market; (2) the third-largest health plan, by enrollment, in the state's small-group market; and (3) the largest national FEHB plan by enrollment across states.

CMS also released additional guidance for certain EHB categories.[24] In a December 2011 bulletin,[25] CMS noted that of the 10 EHB categories, 3 categories were lacking under "typical employer plans." These three categories were pediatric oral and vision services, habilitative services, and mental health and substance use disorder services. To address these issues, CMS outlined a separate supplemental process for pediatric oral and vision services and a separate determination process for habilitative services. Furthermore, CMS released additional guidance in regard to mental health and substance use disorder and prescription drug services.

Pediatric Oral and Vision Services

HHS outlined separate guidelines for supplementing pediatric oral and vision services. An EHBbenchmark plan that does not cover the pediatric oral and vision category is to be supplemented by adding the pediatric oral and/or vision services from either (1) the Federal Employees Dental and Vision Insurance Program (FEDVIP) plan with the largest national enrollment or (2) the benefits from a state's separate Children's Health Insurance Program (CHIP)[26] plan with the highest enrollment, if a separate CHIP plan exists.[27]

For the 2014-2016 coverage years, 49 states and DC had to supplement their EHB-benchmark plans for pediatric oral services—25 states and DC selected a FEDVIP plan, and 24 states selected a CHIP plan as their supplementary plan type (see *Figure 4*). For pediatric vision services, 45 states and DC had to supplement their EHB-benchmark plans; 38 states and DC selected a FEDVIP plan, and 7 states selected a CHIP plan as their supplementary plan type (see *Figure 4*).

Habilitative Services

HHS found that many employer-sponsored plans did not identify habilitative services as a distinct group of services.[28] Thus, in determining habilitative services, HHS proposed policies for coverage of such services.

For the 2014 and 2015 coverage years, the HHS policies allowed states to define the benefits if the EHB-benchmark plan did not include coverage for habilitative services. If a state did not define habilitative services, either plans would have to cover habilitative services benefits that were similar in scope, amount, and duration to benefits covered for rehabilitative services or plans could determine their habilitative services benefits and report them to HHS for review.[29]

For the 2016 coverage year, HHS has modified the habilitative services benefits policy.[30] Rather than allowing plans to cover habilitative services that are offered at parity with rehabilitative services, HHS has adopted a uniform definition for habilitative services. Habilitative services are defined as follows:

> Health care services that help a person keep, learn, or improve skills and functioning for daily living. Examples include therapy for a child who is not walking or talking at the expected age. These services may include physical and occupational therapy, speech-language pathology and other services for people with disabilities in a variety of inpatient and/or outpatient settings.[31]

Although HHS has adopted a definition, states may continue to define habilitative services so long as the state definition complies with EHB policies, including nondiscrimination. Plans, however, no longer may define habilitative services themselves.

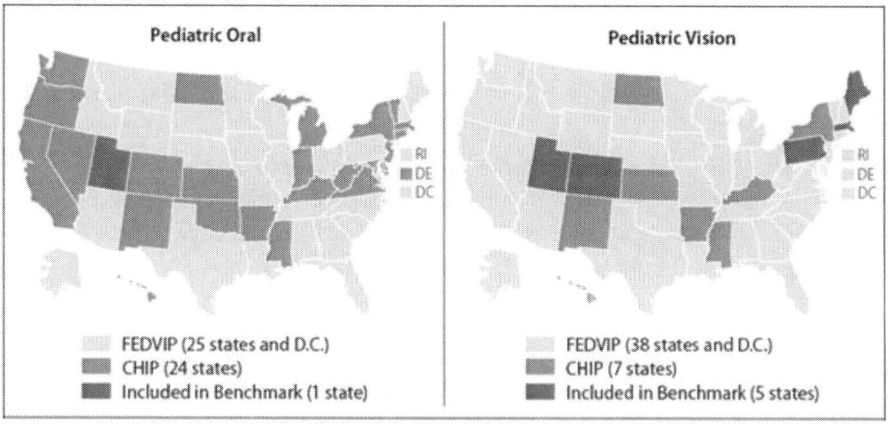

Source: CRS analysis of individual state EHB-benchmark plan summaries provided by Centers for Medicare & Medicaid Services, Additional Information on Proposed State Essential Health Benefits Benchmark Plans, at http://www.cms.gov/CCIIO/Resources/Data-Resources/ehb.html as of May 14, 2015.

Notes: FEDVIP = Federal Employees Dental and Vision Insurance Program. CHIP = Children's Health Insurance Program.

Figure 4. State Selection of Supplementary Plan Types for Pediatric Oral and Vision Services.

Mental Health and Substance Use Disorder Services

For non-group and small-group plans to be EHB compliant, the plans must provide mental health and substance use disorder services, including behavioral health treatment services. These services must be compliant with the Mental Health Parity and Addiction Equity Act (MHPAEA; P.L. 110-343, as amended), which generally requires health insurance coverage for mental health services to be offered on par with covered medical and surgical benefits.

Prescription Drug Services

As part of the EHB, HHS outlined additional requirements regarding prescription drug services. Non-group and small-group market plans must cover *at least* the greater of (1) one drug in every United States Pharmacopeia

(USP) category or class or (2) the same number of prescription drugs in each category and class as the EHB-benchmark plan.[32]

For the 2016 coverage year, HHS finalized additional guidance for the drug exceptions process and formulary drug lists.[33] HHS outlined a drug exceptions process for enrollees to request and gain access to clinically appropriate drugs that are not covered by their health plan. The process takes 72 hours for a standard exception and 24 hours for an expedited review request. If the exception is granted, the plan must treat the drug as an EHB, including counting any cost sharing[34] toward the plan's annual cost-sharing limits.[35] In 2016, plans also must have an up-to-date, accurate, and complete formulary drug list,[36] which must include price tiers, on their websites.[37] The formulary must be easily accessible to plan enrollees, prospective enrollees, the state, the exchange, HHS, the U.S. Office of Personnel Management (OPM), and the general public.

Inclusion of State Benefit Mandates

Prior to the passage of the ACA, many states had laws, known as *state benefit mandates*, that required health plans to cover certain health care services, health care providers, and/or dependents. Examples of state benefit mandates include coverage for substance abuse treatment, chiropractors, or adopted children. A state may require non-group and small-group plans to cover these state benefit mandates in addition to the EHB. Moreover, any state benefit mandates enacted on or before December 31, 2011, are considered to be part of the EHB.[38]

Nonetheless, in addition to covering the EHB, states may choose to impose additional benefit mandates.[39] However, if a state does decide to impose additional benefits, the state itself must defray the cost of those benefits for plans offered in the exchange. The state must make a payment either to the enrollee or directly to the plan on behalf of the enrollee for all plans, regardless of whether an individual is receiving financial assistance.[40] The plan quantifies the cost of the additional benefits. The cost calculation is based on analysis in accordance with generally accepted actuarial principles and methodologies, is conducted by a member of the American Academy of Actuaries, and is reported to the exchange by the plan.

Variation in Essential Health Benefits Coverage

Interstate Variation

Because states selected their own EHB-benchmark plan under the 2014-2016 approach to the EHB, there is considerable variation in EHB coverage from state to state. This variation occurs in terms of specific covered services as well as in terms of amount, duration, and scope. For example, some state EHB-benchmark plans may include bariatric surgery as a covered service whereas other state EHB-benchmark plans may not cover bariatric surgery. In addition, among states that cover bariatric surgery as an EHB, the amount, scope, and duration of the service may vary. For example, the service may be limited to individuals diagnosed as morbidly obese in one state and limited to individuals for whom the service was deemed medically necessary in another state. Additional discussion and illustrative examples of coverage variation from state to state for selected services can be found in table 1. State benefit mandates also may be considered to be part of that state's EHB and thus add to state-level coverage differences.

Intrastate Variation

In addition to EHB variation by state, benefit coverage among plans within a state may differ. States may allow non-group and small-group market plans that offer the EHB to substitute benefits. A benefit may be substituted if the substitution is actuarially[41] equivalent to the benefit being replaced[42] and is made within the same EHB category.[43] For example, a plan could offer coverage of up to 10 physical therapy visits and up to 20 occupational therapy visits as a substitute for EHB-benchmark plan coverage of up to 20 physical therapy visits and 10 occupational therapy visits, assuming actuarial equivalence and the other criteria are met.[44] Substitutions, however, cannot be made for prescription drug benefits.

ESSENTIAL HEALTH BENEFITS FOR 2017

For the 2017 coverage year, the EHB will continue to be defined by the benchmark approach— that is, having states select a reference plan on which most non-group and small-group market plans must substantially base their benefits package. However, for 2017, states will select a new EHB-benchmark plan based on plans available in the 2014 coverage year.[45]

Table 1. Illustrative Examples of Coverage Variation in State Essential Health Benefits Benchmark Plans for Selected Services

Service	Variation
Bariatric Surgery	Fewer than half of state EHB-benchmark plans provide coverage for bariatric surgery. Among state benchmark plans that do cover bariatric surgery services, the coverage itself varies by state. Many state benchmark plans limit bariatric surgery to individuals diagnosed as morbidly obese or to individuals for whom the service was deemed medically necessary. Some benchmark plans have additional limitations on the service, such as one procedure per lifetime or exclusions of certain types of bariatric procedures. Moreover, some plans exclude weight-reduction programs or supplies from the service.
Chiropractic Care	A majority of state EHB-benchmark plans provide coverage for chiropractic care. The benefit description itself varies by state; for example, some states include spinal manipulations with chiropractic care. Chiropractic care coverage varies by benefit amount, ranging from 10 visits to 40 visits per year (with certain exclusions). Some state benchmark plans combine chiropractic care visit limits with rehabilitative, habilitative, and occupational therapy benefit limits.
Home Health Care	All state EHB-benchmark plans provide coverage for home health care services. Nonetheless, coverage varies by amount (e.g., ranging from 20 visits to 150 visits per year; 30 days to 100 days per year; or 28 hours per week). Benefit exclusions vary by benchmark plan. Reimbursement for services provided by a family member, dietician services, and custodial care often are excluded from a plan's home health care benefits.
Infertility Treatment	Fewer than half of state EHB-benchmark plans provide coverage for infertility treatment services. The benefit scope varies by benchmark plans. For example, some plans exclude assistive reproductive

Service	Variation
	technology, artificial insemination, donor eggs, or surrogacy. Furthermore, plans may limit the benefit amount by treatment limits (e.g., one procedure per lifetime or six complete ooctye retrievals per lifetime).

Source: CRS analysis of state EHB-benchmark plan summary information provided by Centers for Medicare & Medicaid Services, "Additional Information on Proposed State Essential Health Benefits Benchmark Plans," at http://www.cms.gov/CCIIO/Resources/Data-Resources/ehb.html as of May 14, 2015.

Note: Examples provided in this table are for illustrative purposes only.

In addition to requiring new EHB-benchmark plans, HHS finalized additional guidance for habilitative services and prescription drug services. (For information on current regulations surrounding these services, see the "Habilitative Services" and "Prescription Drug Services" sections of this report.) For the 2017 coverage year, HHS will require plans to have separate visit limits on habilitative and rehabilitative services.[46] For prescription drug services, HHS will require plans to use a pharmacy and therapeutics (P&T) committee[47] system in addition to the current USP drug count standard. The P&T committees will develop formulary drug lists that cover prescription drugs across a broad range of therapeutic categories and classes and that do not discourage enrollment by any group of consumers. The P&T committees will have to review and approve plan policies that affect consumer access to drugs.[48]

APPLICABILITY OF ESSENTIAL HEALTH BENEFITS REQUIREMENTS TO HEALTH PLANS

Health Plans Subject to Essential Health Benefits Requirements

Generally, non-group and fully insured small-group market health plans are required to offer the EHB. This requirement applies to non-group and small-group plans offered both inside and outside the exchanges. Additional plan types are subject to the EHB (see *Figure 5*).

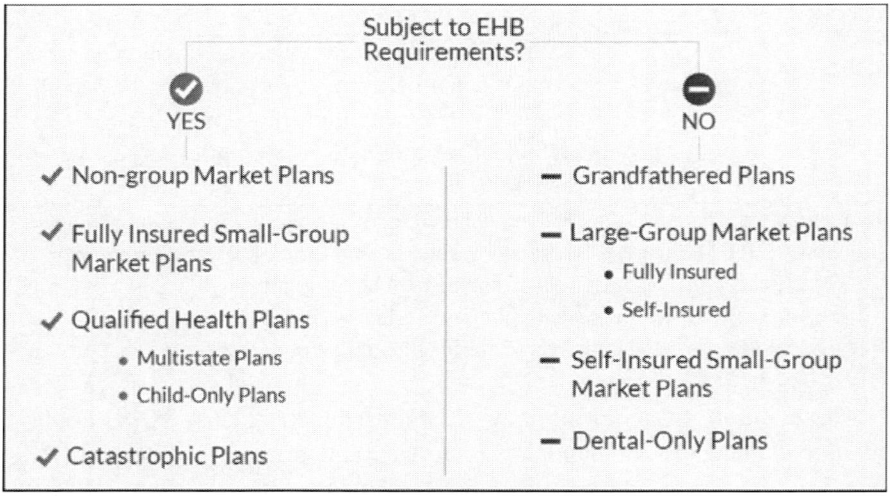

Sources: CRS analysis of 42 U.S.C. §18021 and 42 U.S.C. §18022.

Notes: This figure is not an exhaustive list of existing plan types. Limited exceptions may apply.

Figure 5. Applicability of Essential Health Benefits Requirements to Health Plans.

Qualified Health Plans

The ACA generally requires that non-group and small-group health[49] insurance plans offered through exchanges are Qualified Health Plans (QHPs). Typically, to be a certified as a QHP a plan has to offer the EHB, comply with cost-sharing limits, and meet certain market reforms. Each exchange is responsible for certifying the plans it offers. However, QHPs can be offered both inside the health insurance exchanges and outside the exchanges on the private health insurance market.[50] The exchanges also offer variants of QHPs such as multistate plans and child-only plans.

Multistate Plans

The ACA directs OPM to contract with private insurers in each state to offer at least two[51] comprehensive health insurance options, known as multistate plans (MSPs). MSPs are designed to offer nationally available QHPs through the exchanges; MSPs are not available outside the exchanges. Some MSP options also offer in-network[52] care for out-of-state services, but not all do.

MSPs must offer a package of benefits that includes the EHB (see *Figure 1*). MSPs also must offer a package of benefits that is substantially equal to either the state-selected EHB-benchmark plan for the state in which the plan is offered or an OPM-selected benchmark plan.[53] Moreover, MSPs must comply with any state standards related to benefit mandates, substitution of benefits, and habilitative services.[54]

Child-Only Plans

Child-only health insurance plans are a type of QHP available in the exchanges. To offer child-only plans in an exchange, a health insurance plan must also offer a QHP in the exchange. The ACA requires the plan to offer the child-only exchange plan at the same coverage level as the QHP.[55] Only individuals under the age of 21 may enroll in child-only exchange plans. Child-only health plans are treated as a type of QHP and thus are subject to EHB requirements.[56]

Catastrophic Plans

Catastrophic plans are a type of health plan offered in the individual exchanges. Catastrophic plans offered through exchanges provide the EHB and coverage for at least three primary care visits. The monthly premium for catastrophic plans generally is lower than for other QHPs. However, catastrophic plans impose a very high deductible, and cost sharing generally is higher. These plans also do not meet the minimum requirements related to coverage generosity (i.e., actuarial value).[57] Catastrophic plans may be offered only in the individual market for (1) individuals under the age of 30 and (2) persons exempt from the ACA requirement to obtain health coverage because no affordable coverage is available or they have a hardship exemption.[58]

Health Plans Not Subject to Essential Health Benefits Requirements

Certain health plans are not subject to the EHB requirements. Examples of these health plans include grandfathered plans, large-group market plans, self-insured plans, and dental-only plans (see *Figure 5*).

Grandfathered Plans

Health insurance plans that were in existence (in the non-group, small-group, or large-group market) and in which at least one person was enrolled on the date of the ACA's enactment (March 23, 2010) are considered grandfathered and have a unique status under the ACA. As long as a plan maintains its grandfathered status, the plan has to comply with some but not all

ACA provisions. Grandfathered plans are not subject to the EHB requirements. Plans may lose their status if they apply certain changes to benefits, cost sharing, employer contributions, and access to coverage.[59]

Large-Group Market Plans

Large-group market plans typically are employer-sponsored insurance plans and are defined by the number of employees. In general, a large-group plan has 50 or more employees. Starting with the 2016 coverage year, the ACA requires states to define large-group plans as 100 or more employees.

Many of the market reform provisions in the ACA targeted the non-group and small-group markets. The reforms focused on perceived failures in these markets and provided parity with the large-group market. Accordingly, large-group plans are exempt from a number of ACA market reforms, including coverage of the EHB.[60]

Nonetheless, benefits and coverage offered in large-group market plans play an important role for the EHB. Recall that in defining the EHB, HHS examined the scope of benefits under a typical employer-sponsored insurance plan and used that information in determining what services would be covered as well as additional supplemental guidelines.

Self-Insured Plans

Self-insured plans are a type of group health plan. Organizations that self-insure do not purchase health coverage from insurance carriers. Self-insured plans refer to health coverage that is provided directly by the organization seeking coverage for its members (e.g., a firm providing health benefits to its employees). Such organizations set aside funds and pay for health benefits directly. Under self-insurance, the organization bears the risk for covering medical expenses. Firms that self-insure may contract with third-party administrators to handle administrative duties such as member services, premium collection, and utilization review. Self-insured plans are not subject to many of the ACA market reforms, including the EHB.

Dental-Only Plans

In the exchanges, an individual can obtain dental coverage as part of a QHP or as a stand-alone dental plan. Dental-only plans must provide coverage for pediatric oral services (1 of the 10 EHB categories). Dental-only plans are not required to cover the remaining EHB categories.[61]

ESSENTIAL HEALTH BENEFITS AND OTHER ACA PROVISIONS

Cost Sharing

The ACA imposes an annual cap on consumer cost sharing for the EHB. The ACA specifies that the limits work in two[62] ways: they prohibit (1) applying deductibles to preventive health services and (2) annual out-of-pocket limits that exceed existing limits in the tax code. The cost-sharing limits apply only to in-network benefits and must include all co-payments, coinsurance, and deductibles.[63]

In 2015, the cost-sharing limits are $6,600 for an individual plan and $13,200 for a family plan. For 2016, the cost-sharing limits are $6,850 for an individual plan and $13,700 for a family plan.[64]

Lifetime and Annual Dollar Limits

Prior to the ACA, plans generally were able to set lifetime and annual limits—dollar limits on how much the plan would spend for covered health benefits either during the entire period an individual was enrolled in the plan (lifetime limits) or during a plan year (annual limits). The ACA prohibited both lifetime and annual limits on the EHB. Plans are permitted to place lifetime and annual limits on covered benefits that are not considered EHBs, to the extent that such limits are permitted by federal and state law.[65]

Minimum Essential Coverage

The EHB differs from minimum essential coverage. *Minimum essential coverage* is a term defined in the ACA and its implementing regulations that refers to the *individual mandate,*[66] or the ACA requirement that most individuals must have health insurance coverage for themselves and their dependents or potentially pay a penalty for noncompliance.[67] The definition of minimum essential coverage does not refer to minimum benefits but rather includes most private and public coverage (e.g., employer-sponsored coverage, individual coverage, Medicare, and Medicaid, among others).[68]

End Notes

[1] The non-group (also known as the *individual*) market is where individuals can purchase health coverage directly from an insurer.

[2] What constitutes *small* and *large* in the private market varies. Before enactment of the Patient Protection and Affordable Care Act (ACA;P.L. 111-148, as amended), the dividing line between small and large groups typically was 50 employees. In 2016, the dividing line will increase to 100 employees. Thus, businesses with fewer than 100 employees will be defined as small employers and be eligible for small-group coverage. Until the 100-employee large-group definition takes effect in 2016, the ACA allows states to choose whether to define small employers as those that employ 100 or fewer employees or those that employ 50 or fewer employees.

[3] For more information on the ACA's private health insurance provisions, see CRS Report R43854, *Overview of Private Health Insurance Provisions in the Patient Protection and Affordable Care Act (ACA)*, by Annie L. Mach and Namrata K. Uberoi.

[4] 42 U.S.C. §18022.

[5] For information on what constitutes a grandfathered plan, see the "Grandfathered Plans" section of this report.

[6] Self-insured small-group market health plans are not required to cover the essential health benefits (EHB). For information on what constitutes a self-insured plan, see the "Self-Insured Plans" section of this report.

[7] 42 U.S.C. §18022.

[8] 42 U.S.C. §18022.

[9] 42 U.S.C. §18022.

[10] Centers for Medicare & Medicaid Services, *Essential Health Benefits Bulletin*, December 16, 2011, at https://www.cms.gov/CCIIO/Resources/Files/Downloads/essential_health_benefits_bulletin.pdf.

[11] Department of Labor, *Selected Medical Benefits: A Report from the Department of Labor to the Department of Health and Human Services*, April 15, 2011, at http://www.bls.gov/ncs/ebs/sp/selmedbensreport.pdf.

[12] Institute of Medicine, *Essential Health Benefits: Balancing Coverage and Cost,* October 6, 2011, at https://www.iom.edu/Reports/2011/Essential-Health-Benefits-Balancing-Coverage-and-Cost.aspx.

[13] For more information, see the "Variation in Essential Health Benefits Coverage" section of this report.

[14] The EHB-benchmark approach for the 2014 and 2015 coverage years was finalized in regulation. For more information, see Department of Health and Human Services (HHS), "Patient Protection and Affordable Care Act: Standards Related to Essential Health Benefits, Actuarial Value, and Accreditation," 78 *Federal Register* 12834-12872, February 25, 2013.

[15] The general approach and benchmark selection for the 2016 coverage year did not change from the previous final rule. This continuity in approach is not stated explicitly in the most recent final rule. However, the Congressional Research Service confirmed with HHS that the benchmark selection for the 2016 coverage year has not changed. For more information, see HHS, "Patient Protection and Affordable Care Act: HHS Notice of Benefit and Payment Parameters for 2016," 80 *Federal Register* 10750-10877, February 27, 2015.

[16] See footnote 6 for exception for self-insured small-group market health plans.

[17] The exchanges are marketplaces in which individuals and small businesses can shop for and purchase private health insurance coverage. The ACA requires all states to have two exchanges: (1) an individual exchange and (2) a small business health options program (SHOP) exchange. For more information on the health insurance exchanges, see CRS Report R44065, *Overview of Health Insurance Exchanges*, coordinated by Namrata K. Uberoi.

[18] HHS initially used the Public Health Service Act (PHSA; 78-410) definition of *state* for new PHSA requirements and funding opportunities included in Title I of the ACA. Under this definition, the new market reforms (including coverage of the EHB) in the ACA applied to the U.S. territories (Puerto Rico, Guam, the U.S. Virgin Islands, American Samoa, and the Northern Marina Islands). However, in a letter to the U.S. territories, HHS subsequently determined that U.S. territories do not meet the definition of *state* for purposes of certain market reforms (e.g., EHB). For more information, see http://www.cms.gov/CCIIO/Resources/Letters/Downloads/letter-to-Francis.pdf.

[19] 45 C.F.R. §156.100. A list of these products by state can be found at Centers for Medicare & Medicaid Services, *Essential Health Benefits: List of the Largest Three Small Group Products by State*, July 3, 2012, at https://www.cms.gov/CCIIO/Resources/Files/Downloads/largest-smgroup-products-7-2-2012.pdf.

[20] Ibid.

[21] In the 2014 and 2015 coverage years, when non-group and small-group market health plans in U.S. territories were required to cover the EHB, the default EHB-benchmark plan for U.S. territories was the largest Federal Employees Health Benefits (FEHB) plan.

[22] For more information on each state's EHB-benchmark plan, see benchmark plan summary information provided by Centers for Medicare & Medicaid Services, "Additional Information on Proposed State Essential Health Benefits Benchmark Plans," at http://www.cms.gov/CCIIO/Resources/Data-Resources/ehb.html.

[23] 45 C.F.R. §156.110.

[24] HHS issued guidance for the 2014 and 2015 coverage years as a final rule in HHS, "Patient Protection and Affordable Care Act: Standards Related to Essential Health Benefits, Actuarial Value, and Accreditation," 78 *Federal Register* 12834-12872, February 25, 2013. HHS issued additional guidance for the 2016 coverage year as a final rule in HHS, "Patient Protection and Affordable Care Act: HHS Notice of Benefit and Payment Parameters for 2016," 80 *Federal Register* 10750-10877, February 27, 2015.

[25] Centers for Medicare & Medicaid Services, *Essential Health Benefits Bulletin*, December 16, 2011, at https://www.cms.gov/CCIIO/Resources/Files/Downloads/essential_health_ benefits_bulletin.pdf.

[26] States may design their Children's Health Insurance Programs (CHIP) in three ways: a CHIP Medicaid expansion, a separate CHIP program, or a combination approach in which the state operates a CHIP Medicaid expansion and one or more separate CHIP programs concurrently. CHIP benefit coverage and cost-sharing rules depend on program design. For separate CHIP programs, the benefits are permitted to look more like private health insurance and states may impose cost sharing, such as premiums or enrollment fees.

[27] 45 C.F.R. §156.110.

[28] Laura Skopec, Ashley Henderson, and Susan Todd, et al., *Essential Health Benefits: Comparing Benefits in Small Group Products and State and Federal Employee Plans*, HHS, December 2011, at http://aspe.hhs.gov/health/reports/2011/marketcomparison/rb.pdf.

[29] HHS, "Patient Protection and Affordable Care Act: Standards Related to Essential Health Benefits, Actuarial Value, and Accreditation," 78 *Federal Register* 12834-12872, February 25, 2013.

[30] HHS, "Patient Protection and Affordable Care Act: HHS Notice of Benefit and Payment Parameters for 2016," 80 *Federal Register* 10750-10877, February 27, 2015.

[31] Ibid.

[32] 45 C.F.R. §156.122.

[33] Ibid.

[34] *Cost sharing* is the share of costs an insured individual pays for services; the term often includes deductibles, coinsurance, and co-payments. A *deductible* is the amount an insured individual pays before his or her health insurance issuer begins to pay for services. *Coinsurance* is the share of costs, figured in percentage form, an insured individual pays for a health service. A *co-payment* is a fixed amount an insured individual pays for a health service.

[35] For information on the annual limits on cost sharing, see the "Cost Sharing" section of this report.

[36] A formulary is a list of drugs that a plan chooses to cover and the terms under which those drugs are covered.

[37] Health insurance plans may assign formulary drugs to price tiers that correspond to different levels of cost sharing.

[38] 45 C.F.R. §155.170.

[39] Ibid.

[40] Persons who obtain coverage through the individual exchange may be eligible for financial assistance from the federal government. Eligibility for such assistance is based on income and provided in the form of premium tax credits and cost-sharing subsidies. For more information, see CRS Report R43945, *Health Insurance Premium Credits in the Patient Protection and Affordable Care Act (ACA) in 2015*, by Bernadette Fernandez.

[41] Actuarial value is a summary measure of a plan's generosity of coverage, expressed as a percentage of medical expenses for a standard population and a set of allowed charges estimated to be paid by the issuer. In other words, actuarial values reflect the relative proportions of cost sharing that may be imposed. On average, the lower the actuarial value of a plan, the greater the cost sharing for the enrollee.

[42] The substitutions are based on standards set forth in CHIP regulations at 42 C.F.R. §457.431.

[43] 45 C.F.R. §156.115.

[44] HHS, Centers for Medicare & Medicaid Services, *Frequently Asked Questions on Essential Health Benefits*, February 2012.

[45] HHS, "Patient Protection and Affordable Care Act: HHS Notice of Benefit and Payment Parameters for 2016," 80 *Federal Register* 10750-10877, February 27, 2015. A list of these products by state can be found at Centers for Medicare & Medicaid Services, *Essential Health Benefits: List of the Largest Three Small Group Products by State*, April 8, 2015, at https://www.cms.gov/CCIIO/Resources/Regulations-and-Guidance/Downloads/largest-smgroupproducts-4-8-15-508d-pdf-Adobe-Acrobat-Pro.pdf.

[46] 45 C.F.R. §156.115.

[47] The pharmacy and therapeutics committee is a committee that meets to decide which drugs will appear on a health insurance plan's drug formulary.

[48] 45 C.F.R. §156.122.

[49] There are non-group and small-group health plans offered outside the exchanges that are not QHPs. However, these plans are still required to cover the EHB.

[50] 42 U.S.C. §18021.

[51] One of the issuers must be nonprofit.

[52] The facilities, providers, and suppliers with which a health plan has contracted to provide health care services.

[53] The Office of Personnel Management-selected EHB-benchmark plans are the three largest FEHB plan options. Recall that for the 2014-2016 coverage years, no state selected an FEHB plan as its state EHB-benchmark plan.

[54] 45 C.F.R. §800.105.

[55] Coverage level refers to actuarial value. See footnote 41 for an explanation of actuarial value.

[56] 42 U.S.C. §18022.

[57] While catastrophic plans technically do not meet the generosity requirements for coverage, a catastrophic plan may be considered as meeting such coverage generosity requirements so long as it meets the other catastrophic plan requirements described above.

[58] The ACA requires most individuals to have health insurance coverage or potentially to pay a penalty for noncompliance (i.e., the individual mandate). Some individuals are exempt from the mandate and the penalty. The ACA allows the HHS Secretary to grant hardship exemptions from the individual mandate penalty to anyone determined to have suffered a hardship with respect to the capability to obtain coverage. Examples of circumstances that would allow an individual to receive a hardship exemption include an individual not being eligible for Medicaid based on a state's decision not to carry out the ACA expansion and financial or domestic circumstances that prevent an individual from obtaining coverage. For more information, see CRS Report R41331, *Individual Mandate Under the ACA*, by Annie L. Mach.

[59] For information about grandfathered plans, see CRS Report R41166, *Grandfathered Health Plans Under the Patient Protection and Affordable Care Act (ACA)*, by Bernadette Fernandez.

[60] For more information about the applicability of market reforms to health plans, see CRS Report R42069, *Private Health Insurance Market Reforms in the Affordable Care Act (ACA)*, by Annie L. Mach and Bernadette Fernandez.

[61] 42 U.S.C. §18031.

[62] The ACA previously limited cost sharing in three ways. It also included deductible limits for plans offered in the small-group market—generally prohibiting these plans from having deductibles greater than $2,000 for self-only coverage and $4,000 for any other coverage in 2014. However, the Protecting Access to Medicare Act of 2014 (P.L. 113-93) repealed this provision, thereby removing the deductible limits for plans offered in the small-group market.

[63] 45 C.F.R. §156.130.

[64] HHS, "Patient Protection and Affordable Care Act: HHS Notice of Benefit and Payment Parameters for 2016," 80 *Federal Register* 10750-10877, February 27, 2015.

[65] 42 U.S.C. §300gg–11.

[66] For more information, see footnote 58.

[67] 56 U.S.C. §5000A.

[68] For more information on minimum essential coverage see CRS Report R41331, *Individual Mandte Under the ACA*, by Annie L. Mach.

In: Private Health Insurance and Essential Health… ISBN: 978-1-63484-819-0
Editor: Cheryl Bennett

Chapter 3

DRIVERS OF PREMIUM INCREASES AND REVIEW OF HEALTH INSURANCE RATES*

Bernadette Fernandez

SUMMARY

In general, the premiums charged by health insurance companies represent actuarial estimates of the amount that would be required to cover three main components: (1) the expected cost of the health benefits covered under the plan, (2) the business administrative costs of operating the plan, and (3) a profit. The final premium calculation often is adjusted upward or downward to reflect several factors, such as making up for a previous financial loss, that are often referred to as the "underwriting cycle."

Health insurance premiums have been trending up, while the value of coverage generally has been trending down. Specifically, the year-over-year percentage increase by month in private health insurance premiums has averaged around 4.4% between 2004 and 2010, but has accelerated some since 2009, ranging from 4.8% to 5.5%. At the same time, cost-sharing requirements have generally increased. For example, a typical family of four with private employer-sponsored health benefits

* This is an edited, reformatted and augmented version of a Congressional Research Service publication R41588, prepared for Members and Committees of Congress, dated January 20, 2012.

has seen its out-of-pocket cost sharing increase between 5.4% and 10.5% annually between 2006 and 2010.

Of the main components that constitute the premium amount, health benefits expenses represented about 85% of that amount in 2010. Publicly available data indicate that medical costs have steadily risen over the past several years, but the rate of growth in these expenses slowed between 2008 and 2010. The data also suggest that the rise in medical costs is primarily attributable to the price of services, not increased utilization.

The rise in the cost of health insurance has received considerable attention by Congress and resulted in calls for more regulation. The regulation of private health insurance has traditionally been under the jurisdiction of the states. Most states have used their regulatory authority over the business of insurance to require the filing of health insurance documents containing rate information for one or more insurance market segments or plan types.

Under the Patient Protection and Affordable Care Act (P.L. 111-148, ACA, as amended), the federal government will assume a role in private health insurance rate reviews by providing grants to states and requiring health insurance companies to provide justifications for proposed rate increases determined to be unreasonable. However, ACA does not authorize the federal government to decline or bar implementation of proposed rate increases; such authority still is retained by the states. On May 23, 2011, Health and Human Services (HHS) issued the final rule implementing the rate review provisions in ACA. The rule clarified which proposed rate increases would be subject to review (i.e., defining "unreasonable" rate increase), established a process for rate review to be conducted either by the state or HHS, and specified notice requirements to inform the public about the process and outcome of the rate reviews.

This report provides an overview of the concepts, regulation, and available public data regarding private health insurance premiums. Specifically, this report analyzes the four broad components of health insurance premiums: medical claims, administrative costs, profit, and the underwriting cycle. Finally, the report discusses state requirements to review health insurance rates, and rate review provisions under federal health reform.

INTRODUCTION

Health insurance premiums represent a contractually agreed upon amount to be paid for a defined set of health benefits during a defined period of time (usually a year). Premiums are typically paid in monthly installments by policyholders (individual coverage) and enrollees (group coverage). Premiums may vary for different individuals with the same health benefits package from the same insurance company. Each variation is referred to as a premium rate. Rating methodologies generally vary between health insurance market segments and may have additional state-specific variation due to differences in state rate regulations.[1] Typically, the following methods are used by market segment:

- *Individual health insurance market.* Rates may vary by age and sex and may also be underwritten, meaning that the insurance carrier assesses the health status of the insurance applicant and uses it to set the rate according to the health risk of that individual.
- *Small group market.* What is called a "manual rate" is first calculated estimating the costs by the age and sex of the employees, geographic location, number of employees, and the type of health insurance product.[2] Most states also permit the manual rate to be adjusted by a health status factor.
- *Large group market.* Premium rates are determined either from an individual group's medical claims history (referred to as "experience") or from a blended average of manual rates calculated from the members of the group and from the group's experience.[3]

Health insurance premium rates are actuarial estimates of the cost of covering a risk pool of individuals under a particular health benefits package for a particular period of time.[4] Generally, the more generous the benefits package (i.e., large, open networks of providers and low cost- sharing requirements including deductibles) the higher the premiums will be. Just as premiums must be adequate to pay for expected health care use, they also must be sufficient to compensate insurance carriers for taking on the financial risk associated with providing coverage.

The final premium rate calculation often is adjusted to reflect several other factors, such as making up for a previous financial loss and providing excess capital to manage various risks generally regulated under state solvency standards. State regulators have adopted solvency standards to protect consumers by requiring insurance companies to keep certain reserves of capital to protect against asset risks, underwriting or insurance risk, and business risks.[5] Without this required safety net of reserved cash, a health insurance company could go bankrupt if it experiences unforeseen losses, thus resulting in its consumers being placed at full financial risk for their medical claims.

Data from the Bureau of Labor Statistics' (BLS's) Producer Price Index (PPI) for health insurance companies indicates that the year-over-year percentage increase by month in private health insurance premiums has averaged around 4.4% between 2004 and 2010, but has accelerated some since 2009, ranging from 4.8%-5.5% (*Figure 1*).[6]

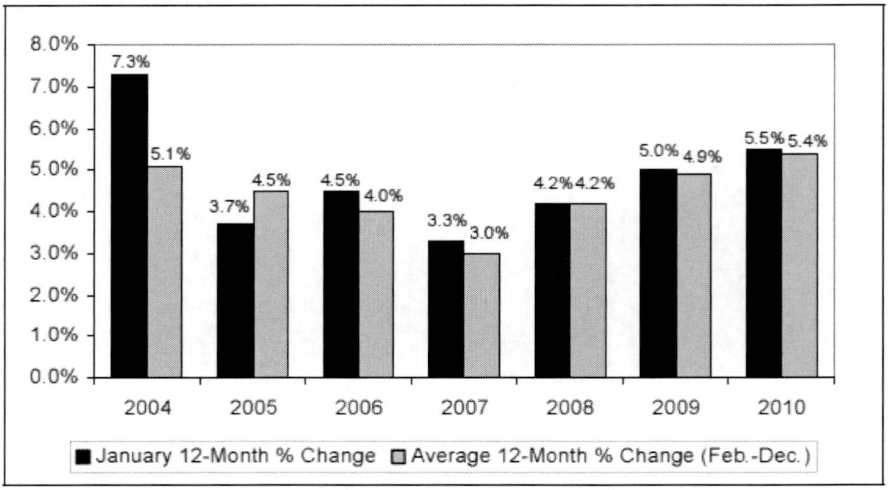

Source: U.S. Department of Labor, Bureau of Labor Statistics (BLS), "Producer Price Index Industry Data," 2010, available at http://data.bls.gov/PDQ/servlet/SurveyOutputServlet?series_id=PCU524114524114.

Notes: The year-over-year percentage change is isolated for January because most group plans are sold for 12- month durations beginning on January 1 of each year. Individual market health insurance products are sold monthly and usually for a 12-month duration. Thus, the average monthly year-over-year % change for February through December is presented. The indexes for this industry measure the change in the total premium (employee and employer contribution) paid to the insurer plus the return on the invested portion of the premium. For more information on the survey methodology, see U.S. Department of Labor, Bureau of Labor Statistics (BLS), "Producer Price Index for the Direct Health and Medical Insurance Carriers Industry – NAICS 524114," September 2005, available at http://www.bls.gov/ppi/ppimedicalinsurance.htm.

Figure 1. Year-Over-Year Percentage Change in Premiums for January and Average for All Other Months, 2004-2010.

The year-to-year increases in the PPI may not appear significant, but there are four relevant contextual factors to take into consideration.

- First, premium increases can be much higher in the individual and small group markets, where the smaller risk pools can result in distortions in the average health care costs covered by premiums, due to outlier policyholders or members. In other words, if there are only a few healthy persons to help pay for a sick person, the premiums (all else being equal) will be higher than if that sick person was in a larger risk pool with many healthy persons.
- Second, in the employer group market, the worker share of premiums has been increasing even more because employer subsidies have been trending down incrementally.[7] The employer and workers shares vary according to coverage tier: self-only, employee-plus-one, and family. However, in the past few years employers have shifted incrementally more of that cost to workers. For example, the average worker share of the total premium for group coverage (for self-only coverage) was 15.3% in 2008 and grew to 17.0% by 2011 (table 1).
- Third, as premiums have gone up, the value of the coverage has gone down in terms of higher cost sharing requirements, including deductibles (see the *Appendix*).
- Fourth, real income (i.e., income adjusted for inflation), both per capita and family, has decreased in the past several years. Real income for adults (age 16 and older) *declined* 4.6%, from an average of $40,389 in 2007 to $38,543 in 2010. Similarly, average family income *declined* 6.6%, from $73,426 to 68,599 for the same period.[8] As a result, incomes are not keeping up with premium increases, and a greater proportion of incomes are being consumed by health insurance premiums.[9]

Table 1. Average Employer and Worker Shares of Total Premiums, by Tier of Coverage, 2008-2011

	2008	2009	2010	2011
Self-Only Coverage				
Employer Share	84.7%	83.9%	82.2%	83.0%
Worker Share	15.3%	16.1%	17.8%	17.0%
Family of Four Coverage				
Employer Share	73.5%	73.7%	71.0%	72.6%
Worker Share	26.5%	26.3%	29.0%	27.4%

Source: Employer Health Benefits, 2011, Kaiser Family Foundation/Health Research and Educational Trust, September 2011.

The growth of health insurance premiums (and out-of-pocket costs) for individuals and families has been the focus of considerable congressional attention.[10] Using available public data, this report explores the potential drivers of the growth trend in health insurance premiums.[11]

DRIVERS OF PREMIUM INCREASES

In general, the premiums charged by health insurance companies represent the estimated amount that would be required to cover initially three major components: (1) the expected cost of the health benefits covered, (2) the administrative costs of operating the coverage, and (3) a profit margin consistent with the strategic business goals of the company.[12] The fourth and final component to the premium calculation involves adjustments upward or downward to reflect several miscellaneous factors, such as responding to prior gains or losses, strategically responding to competitors (i.e., pricing lower to gain market share), hedging against uncertainty risks created by a changing regulatory environment, and other factors often collectively described as the underwriting cycle.

Health Benefits Expenses

Health benefits expenses equal the aggregate products of unit prices for health services times utilization of health services (e.g., hospital visits) or health items, such as prescription drugs. Health benefits expenses represent the largest component of premiums. According to the aggregate health insurance industry statements of revenue and expenses submitted to the National Association of Insurance Commissioners (NAIC) in 2010, health benefits represented about 85% of premiums.[13]

Health benefits expenses on a per member per month (PMPM)[14] basis have trended upwards between 2003 and 2010 in aggregate for the health insurance industry,[15] as illustrated in *Figure 2*. The annual percentage increase in total health benefits expenses, typically referred to as medical trend, has generally been over 7% per year during most of that time period, but the rate of growth was 5.0% between 2008 and 2009, and only 1.1% between 2009 and 2010. The medical trend of a particular plan or policy can vary substantively based on such factors as the relative health status of the enrollees and policyholders, differences in coverage policy, differences in the use of managed care techniques, geographic differences, use of restrictive versus open provider networks, and various organizational factors, such as being for-profit or non-profit.

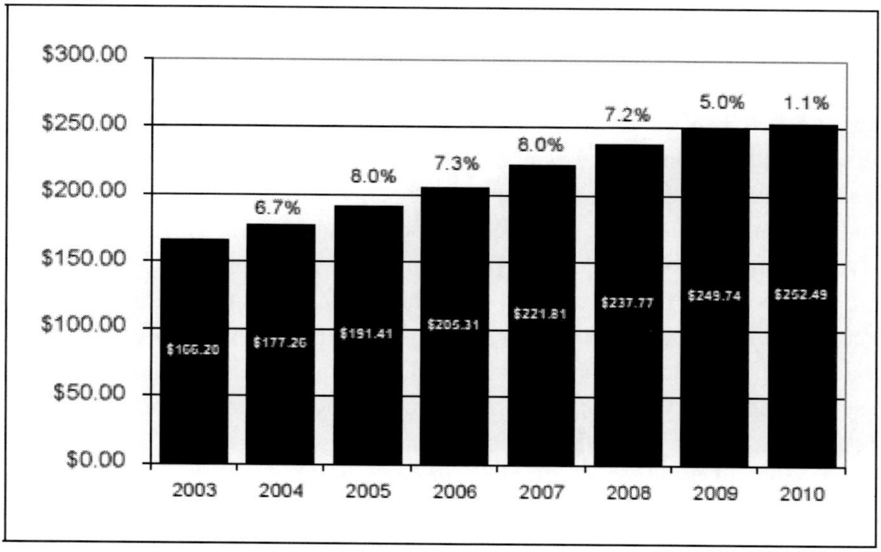

Source: Debra Donahue, "Medical Expense Trend Declines in 2010," September 23, 2011, available at http://www.markfarrah.com/healthcarebs.asp?article=103.

Notes: This study was based on a representative sample of 356 health plans and insurance products from 171 different companies. Only companies that filed Health Annual Statements with the National Association of Insurance Commissioners for each year displayed were included in this analysis. Excluded from the dataset were California HMOs and self-insured health plans that are not required to file Annual Statements with the National Association of Insurance Commissioners (NAIC) and specialty, non-medical plans such as dental insurers. The health benefit expenses are nominal amounts; i.e., not adjusted for inflation.

Figure 2. Per Member Per Month (PMPM) and Annual Percentage Increases in Health Benefits Expenses for the Health Insurance Industry, 2003-2010.

Unit Prices

The unit price of health services and prescription drugs is determined through a contract negotiation process between health insurance companies, health providers, medical device companies, and drug manufacturers or distributors. There is evidence of considerable geographic variation in provider, but not prescription drug pricing.[16] For example, the Center for Studying Health System Change (HSC) found significant differences in payment rates to hospitals and physicians among the eight markets it studied during site visits to nationally representative metropolitan areas during 2010. Average payments for inpatient hospital care, as a percentage of Medicare, ranged from 147% in Miami to 210% in San Francisco. For physician payments as a percentage of Medicare, it ranged from 82% in Miami to 176% in rural Wisconsin.[17] HSC attributed the variation in prices paid by insurers to differences in provider bargaining power. Another study in six California markets between October and December 2008 found that physician group practice integration with hospital systems, hospital mergers, the desire for broad provider choice, growing physician shortages, and a regulatory environment that favors providers all contributed to a price negotiation advantage for some providers.[18]

The power of providers in negotiating higher unit prices has been recognized by some state insurance commissioners that perform premium rate reviews. For example, in the reformed Massachusetts market, the Division of Insurance approved (on appeal) a premium rate increase for Fallon Community Health Plan after finding that, among other things, "individuals and employer groups demand that Fallon provide options that include access to every doctor and hospital, including local providers, as well as access to larger tertiary systems."[19] The Massachusetts Division of Insurance Appeals Board concluded that "[m]arketplace realities mean that Fallon sometimes has no choice but to contract with higher cost providers." Similarly, an investigation by the state Attorney General concluded that large providers with brand-name recognition have considerable leverage over health insurance companies when negotiating prices, and that price increases have accounted for the majority of the medical trend in Massachusetts.[20]

Health care services and items in the United States generally lack unit price transparency because they are considered proprietary contractual negotiations between payers and providers.[21] Moreover, standard measures of producer price inflation, such as the PPI, are inappropriate to examine the unit price inflation among privately insured persons because they include prices paid by consumers that are uninsured or are in government programs (e.g., Medicare and Medicaid). However, one survey by Segal Consulting projected that the annual price inflation for hospitals will increase 7.2% for 2012 (2012 estimates from insurers are based on provider-contracted rates set before the coverage year begins).[22] In addition, Segal projected that the annual price inflation for physicians and prescription drugs in 2012 would be 4.6% and 5.5%, respectively.

Health Service Utilization

Conventional wisdom states that the aging of the American population is the primary driver of increased demand for health services and prescriptions drugs experienced by health insurers.[23] On its face, this seems logical given that the elderly have the highest utilization of health care.[24] However, the overall age distribution of the population actually shifts very slowly over time. Indeed, the median age of the U.S. population is projected to increase just 1.8 years, from 36.9 in 2010 to 38.7 in 2030.[25] In terms of risk based on age, the Medicare program assists the private health insurance market by assuming the liability of coverage for most persons age 65 and older. Ultimately, what matters for the insurer is not merely the general population trends, but the specific age distribution of the risk pool being insured. Moreover, studies have found that while aging does have an impact on rising health care utilization, other factors such as advances in costly medical technology and medical practice patterns drive demand more.[26]

Without countervailing regulations, health insurance companies have a financial incentive to restrain utilization. Generally, the less they pay in health benefits, the higher their profits will be. Health insurance companies can implement a number of different management techniques or limitations on coverage to restrain health care utilization. Traditional utilization management techniques include utilization review, case management, and physician gatekeeping.[27] Insurers may also attempt to limit the use of high-priced or high-utilizing health care providers through their network contracting process. Since the cost sharing is lower for in-network providers, the plan can financially incentivize its members to use lower-cost providers by contracting only with them.[28] Finally, insurers may choose to not cover a particular procedure, use of a technology, or prescription drug.

Generally, utilization management techniques and restrictive benefits became prevalent in the late 1980s, but their use has been waning since the mid-1990s, in the face of strong consumer resistance to anything other than case management, where coordination between providers and evidence based medicine are used to improve outcomes.[29] For example, in the employer group market, enrollment in health maintenance organizations (HMOs), the most restrictive type of plan, dropped from 31% in 1996 to 17% in 2011, while less restrictive preferred provider organization (PPO)/point of service (POS)[30] plans increased from 42% to 65% during the same time period.[31] In the individual (non-group) market, 2009 data from American's Health Insurance Plans (AHIP) indicate that 82.8% of members with single coverage and 72.9% with family coverage elect a PPO/POS plan, with less than 2% electing HMO or similarly restrictive plans.[32]

As the market has moved away from health insurance products with strong utilization management programs and limited provider networks, utilization of health services and prescription drugs has consistently increased every year, as measured in population-based surveys and gross sales figures.[33] These trends in gross measures of service utilization could be explained by increases in the total population or the number of persons that are insured. In other words, per insured member service utilization may not be increasing. However, studies where researchers have had access to claims data and provider payment rates have found that most of the increase in health benefits expenditures, other than certain outpatient procedures and prescription drugs, are attributable to increases in unit prices, not to increases in the utilization per insured member.[34]

Administrative Costs

In addition to paying for medical claims, premiums are expected to cover the operational costs of the insurance company. Health insurance companies generally are complex organizations requiring specialized human resources and information technology to perform the functions of developing, marketing, and operating a health plan or insurance policy. Table 2 provides a summary review of administrative functions in health insurance plans.

Table 2. Summary of Health Insurance Administrative Functions

Account and Member Administration	Corporate Services	Marketing and Sales	Provider & Medical Management
Claims processing	Finance and accounting	Market research	Provider contracting
Member enrollment	Actuarial	Advertising	Utilization management
Customer service	Risk management	Sales to employer groups	Quality improvement
Information technology	Legal and compliance	Sales to individuals	Wellness programs
Member communications	Executives/management	Promotions	Pharmacy management
Account management	Governance (Board)	Underwriting	Provider services

Source: Adapted from the work of Sherlock Company on administrative costs in health plans, available at http://www.sherlockco.com/.

Insurance companies report administrative costs, on a per member per month (PMPM) basis, in regulatory filings. Such data indicate a relatively stable trend, with average costs per company increasing about $3 PMPM from 2007 to 2009 (*Figure 3*).

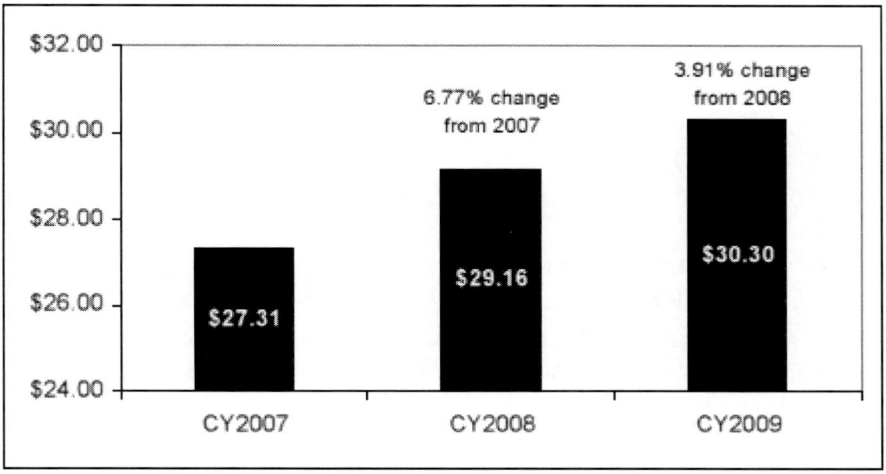

Source: HighlineData's Insurance Analyst Pro database of health insurer regulatory filings.

Notes: Includes 673 different legal entities reporting in all three years with at least 1,000 enrollees. Legal entities with less than 1,000 enrollees were excluded because they typically were startup companies with outlier cost structures. A legal entity refers to an incorporated business licensed to sell insurance. Many large corporate parent organizations have multiple legal entities. For example, Aetna has 16 different companies within this dataset.

Figure 3. Average Health Insurer Administrative Costs Per Company, 2007-2009 (Per Member Per Month).

However, while *average* administrative costs have been relatively consistent, there is more substantial variation across the companies observed. Specialty firms (e.g., dental only, behavioral health) generally report below $10 PMPM in administrative costs, and companies with an emphasis on non-group insurance often report more than $100 PMPM in such costs. Administrative expenses have been found to vary by market segment, with non-group insurance costing the highest and large group the lowest.[35] This is attributable to factors such as enrollment size. While group plans can sell to multiple individuals (for example, through an employer's human resources department), non-group insurance must be sold one-by-one to each person, thus increase marketing and sales costs.

A company with multiple products generally prices each product separately. As an example from a different industry, a car company does not have one price for each of its vehicles. It charges separate prices for each car model, even if the different models are sold in the same year. Similarly, premium rates are calculated at the health insurance product level (i.e., the health plan or policy that a person, family, or employer purchases), not at the company or corporate parent levels (i.e., the corporate entity that sells the insurance product).[36] So additional variation might be observed within each company if product level data were publicly available.

These data are also limited by the fact that many health insurance companies have multiple non-insurance businesses. For example, the United Health Group (UHG) includes the information technology and consulting firm Ingenix and the pharmacy benefits manager (PBM) Prescription Solutions in addition to its health insurance benefits business segment.[37] The inherent complexity of a large conglomerate may create unique challenges for accurate cost accounting down to the individual plans and insurance products sold within the organization. These challenges could create barriers to fair and comprehensive regulation of administrative costs across different types of health insurance companies (i.e., small local and regional non-profit insurers versus large national investor-owned, for-profit insurers).

There is no consensus benchmark for what is an appropriate amount of administrative costs. Nevertheless, several industry executives of the publicly traded for-profit firms believe that administrative costs can come down as evidenced in the summary of recent earnings conference calls provided in table 3.

Table 3. Quotes from Health Insurance Executives about Administrative Costs

Executive's Name and Organization	Quotes Concerning Administrative Costs
Allen Wise, CEO of Coventry Health Care	During 2009, we spent time addressing the administrative cost structure for these areas and improvement will continue during 2010. While I can't predict where changes in government involvement will go there are certain things we can and must do everyday. We can better

Executive's Name and Organization	Quotes Concerning Administrative Costs
	manage our cost structure and we will. This includes both medical and [selling, general, and administrative (SG&A) expenses].
James Bloem, Senior Vice President and CFO of Humana	Our cross-functional administrative costs committee has developed processes which assure that these administrative cost reduction efforts are not just one time events, but rather an ongoing source of both improved cost competitiveness and savings-funded initiatives.
Michael Neidorff, Chairman, President, and CEO of Centene Corporation	Further [general and administrative (G&A) expense] reduction beyond 2010 remains a top priority, and our ongoing systems investments should enable us to accomplish this goal.
Angela Braly, Chair, President, and CEO of Wellpoint Inc.	Another key to our continued success in the future will be the ability to generate even greater administrative efficiency as an organization. We currently have one of the leading SG&A cost structures within our industry, and we have plans and programs in place to further improve upon this position.
Ronald Williams, CEO of Aetna	As we go forward in 2011, we understand the need to bring our SG&A down.

Sources: Allen Wise, "Coventry 4th Quarter 2009 Earnings Call," February 9, 2010, available at http://seekingalpha.com/article/187560-coventry-health-care-inc-q4-2009-earnings-call-transcript?page=-1&find= coventry. James Bloem, "Humana 4th Quarter 2010 Earnings Call," February 7, 2011, available at http://seekingalpha.com/article/251330-humana-s-ceo-discusses-q4-2010-results-earnings-call-transcript. Michael Neidorff, "Centene 4th Quarter 2009 Earnings Call," February 9, 2010, available at http://seekingalpha.com/article/187587-centene-corporation-q4-2009-earnings-call-transcript?page=-1. Wayne DeVeydt, "Wellpoint 4th Quarter Earnings Call," January 27, 2010, available at http://seekingalpha.com/article/184862-wellpoint-inc-q4-2009-earnings-call-transcript?page=-1. Ronald Williams, "Aetna 2nd Quarter 2010 Earnings Call," July 29, 2010, available at http://seekingalpha.com/article/217209-aetna-q2-2010-earnings-call-transcript.

Note: The term "SG&A" means selling, general, and administrative and is reported on the income statement, it is the sum of all direct and indirect selling expenses and all general and administrative expenses of a company.

Health Insurance Company Profits

The average profit margin for the health insurance industry has consistently been low; therefore, profit typically represents the smallest component of health insurance premiums. According to financial data submitted to the NAIC, the average profit margin (net income divided by total revenues) for the health insurance industry was 3.5% in 2010.[38] Because of the membership scale associated with more profitable health insurers, it is unlikely that reductions in net income would have a substantive impact on premiums for individual members. For example, if WellPoint's entire 2010 net income of $2.89 billion were rebated back to its 2010 members, it would result in a monthly credit of $7.22 per member.[39]

There is substantial variation in health insurance company profits due to differences in the size of the companies, their willingness to aggressively manage health costs, and other business goals of the organization. Wellpoint, a large (33.3 million members) investor-owned, national for-profit company, emphasizes reduced costs and value for its investors. [40] In 2010, Wellpoint had $2.89 billion in net income (profits after taxes). By contrast, Blue Cross Blue Shield of Rhode Island (BCBS-RI), a mid-sized (approximately 600,000 members) non-profit company operating in one state with a community mission, took a $14.1 million loss in 2010.[41]

The Underwriting Cycle

The health insurance underwriting cycle refers to the tendency for health insurance premiums and insurer profitability to cycle over certain time intervals.[42] (This is a different, but related, concept to medical underwriting, which is the process by which an insurer estimates the insurance risks and potential medical costs associated with an applicant for insurance based on characteristics of that applicant.) Upturns and downturns in the underwriting cycle are basically the outcome of adjustments to premiums that reflect past experience, expectations of future losses, business strategy, attempts to mitigate possible impacts of regulatory changes, and the changing demands of plan participants and policyholders (e.g., demand for large and open provider networks). For example, a health insurance company may charge premiums above the anticipated amount necessary for the current plan year's costs because the insurer lost money on the product in previous years. This will start an up cycle in profitability until it prices itself out of the competitive market, thus forcing a cut in premiums and ultimately profit margins. Alternatively, the insurer may have a business strategy to obtain as much market share as possible. To do this, the insurer reduces premiums below competitors, even if it reduces profit margins or results in a temporary loss. Once the insurer commands the desired market share, it increases premiums to achieve the desired maximum profit margin that the market will allow.

Adding to the complexity, the insurance company often may attempt to subsidize one policy or plan with profits from another. To illustrate this, table 4 provides an example of one insurance carrier's actual premium and medical loss experience in one state between 2007 and 2009. The table was abstracted from a premium rate increase request for 2010 for individual market blocks of business with and without maternity coverage from Anthem Blue Cross Life and Health Insurance Company (hereafter referred to as "Anthem") submitted to the California Department of Insurance. For the years 2007 through 2009, the table presents the actual per member per month (PMPM) premiums charged, the PMPM claims experience, the medical loss ratio (the percentage of premiums spent on medical claims), the total member months, and the gain or loss on medical expenses by the maternity and non-maternity blocks of business in the individual (non-group) market. Member months are used to reflect enrollment based metrics because individuals can join or leave a plan or policy on a monthly basis. Thus, having a member for 6 months versus the full year (12 member months) would be meaningful in terms of total premiums collected and likely claims experience.

Anthem's maternity coverage policies had an operational gain in 2007, with relatively few policyholders (in member months). However, these policies operated at a loss in 2008 and 2009 despite a higher number of policyholders. Based on this trend, Anthem projected nearly a $14.2 million loss for 2010 on the maternity block of business. What are some of the options for Anthem or any other insurance company in a situation like this? It could increase premiums in the maternity coverage policies to $320 PMPM to match expected claims costs PMPM for 2010, but that would be nearly a 74% increase from premiums in 2009. Alternatively, Anthem could eliminate the maternity coverage policies, seek out non-premium sources of revenue (e.g., investment income), aggressively implement managed care methods to reduce costs, or make up for the losses in this product with gains from another product line.[43] The latter option is what is suggested by this data. In other words, losses from the maternity coverage are financially cancelled out for the company by gains from the policies sold without maternity coverage.

Table 4. Anthem Individual Health Insurance Rates for Policies in California

With or Without Maternity Coverage

Coverage	Actual or projected	Year	Premium PMPM	Claims PMPM	Medical Loss Ratio	Member Months	Gain/Loss on Medical Expenses
	Actual	2007	$179	$108	60%	12,141	$862,011.00
Maternity	Actual	2008	$184	$217	118%	64,348	-$2,123,484.00
Coverage	Actual	2009	$184	$268	146%	105,490	-$8,861,160.00
	Projected	2010	$195	$320	164%	113,340	-$14,167,500.00
	Actual	2007	$116	$309	266%	89	-$17,177.00
No	Actual	2008	$130	$66	51%	61,271	$3,921,344.00
Maternity							
Coverage	Actual	2009	$141	$86	61%	205,371	$11,295,405.00
	Projected	2010	$154	$111	72%	329,486	$14,167,898.00

Source: Anthem Blue Cross Life and Health Insurance Company, "Rate for Individual Policies," submitted to the California Department of Insurance June 30, 2010, available at http://www.insurance.ca.gov/0250-insurers/IndHlthRateFilings/upload/AnthemCHDPPF201002158.pdf.

Notes: The acronym PMPM stands for per member per month. The term "medical loss ratio" means the percentage of premium revenue spent on medical claims. The term "member month" refers to each month of coverage for an enrollee or policyholder, thus a member for a full year would have 12 member months. Gain/Loss on medical expenses refers to the gain or loss experienced from paying medical claims out of premium revenues. This calculation does not involve other financial factors such as administrative costs.

REVIEW OF HEALTH INSURANCE RATES

The regulation of private health insurance has traditionally been under the jurisdiction of the states.[44] Most states have used their regulatory authority over the business of insurance to require the filing of health insurance documents containing rate information for one or more market segments or plan types.[45] Under the Patient Protection and Affordable Care Act (P.L. 111-148, ACA, as amended), the federal government assumed a role in health insurance rate reviews by providing grant funding to states for such reviews and requiring, among other things, that insurers justify rate increases under certain circumstances.

State Rate Filing and Reviews

As the primary regulators of health insurance, states oversee many aspects of the industry concerning the insurance products offered in the market and the entities that sell insurance. One fundamental area in which states exercise regulatory authority is through the imposition of rate and form filing requirements. "Form" refers to the language in the insurance contract and typically is required when a new plan is offered in the market (or changes are made to that plan). "Rate" refers to the price of a unit of insurance.[46] Rates are filed with the initial form and usually must be filed each time an insurance carrier proposes to change rates for a plan (or if changes in the form filing affect rates).

Not all states actually conduct rate reviews. For those states that do, the purpose is threefold: to ensure that rates are sufficient (to guard against insolvency), but not too high (must be actuarially justified), nor unfairly discriminatory (variation in rates must be based on differences in expected claims). There is substantive variation in state regulation of health insurance rates. Some states collect rates for informational purposes only or as part of their form filing requirements. Over half of states have "prior approval" requirements, where insurance companies must file proposed rate changes and the state has the authority to approve, disapprove or modify the request. However, prior approval authority typically also includes a deeming period; if the state does not take any action and the deeming period elapses, the filing become effective. Under such a scenario, prior approval requirements may effectively work just like "file and use." File and use requires insurers to file rates with the state, which become effective either immediately or on a date specified in the filing. Under either of these scenarios, the state may disapprove a rate filing if it does not meet a certain compliance standard, such as a minimum anticipated medical loss ratio. Several states have file and use requirements. One state has "use and file," which means the filing becomes effective when used, though the insurer is required to file rates with the state. (A list of rate filing requirements by state is provided in table 5.)

Table 5. State Rate Filing Requirements, by Market Segment, 2010

State	No Requirement	File with Form	Information Only	Use and File	File and Use	Prior Approval
Alabama			I, S, L			
Alaska						I, S, L
Arizona	S, L		I			
Arkansas	S, L					I
California					I, S, L	
Colorado						I, S, L
Connecticut						I, S, L
Delaware					I, S, L	
Florida						I, S, L
Georgia			I, S, L			
Hawaii						I, S, L
Idaho	S, L				I	
Illinois	S, L	I				
Indiana					S, L	I
Iowa						I, S, L
Kansas					I, S, L	
Kentucky					I, S, L	
Louisiana					I, S, L	
Maine					I, S, L[a]	
Maryland						I, S, L
Massachusetts	S[b], L[b]					I
Michigan	S, L				I	
Minnesota						I, S, L
Mississippi			I, S, L			
Missouri	I, S, L					
Montana	I, S, L					
Nebraska		S, L			I	
Nevada	S, L				I	
New Hampshire					L	I, S
New Jersey	S[c], L[c]					I
New Mexico						I, S,L
New York[d]					I, S, L[a]	10/1/2010 forward
North Carolina						I, S, L

Table 5. (Continued)

State	No Requirement	File with Form	Information Only	Use and File	File and Use	Prior Approval
North Dakota						I, S, L
Ohio						I, S, L
Oklahoma		I, S, L				
Oregon					L	I, S
Pennsylvania						I, S, L
Rhode Island						I, S, L
South Carolina	S, L					I
South Dakota	S, L				I	
Tennessee						I, S, L
Texas					I, S, L	
Utah					I, S, L	
Vermont						I, S, L
Virginia			S, L			I
Washington						I, S, L
West Virginia						I, S, L
Wisconsin				I, S, L		
Wyoming	I, S, L					
Washington D.C.						I, S, L

Sources: National Association of Insurance Commissioners (NAIC), "State Rate Filing Requirements by Market Segment," February 2009; National Association of Insurance Commissioners, "NAIC Response to Request for Information Regarding Section 2794 of the Public Health Service Act," May 12, 2010; and New York State, Office of the Governor, "Governor Paterson Signs Landmark Health Insurance Reform Legislation," June 9, 2010.

Notes: I – Individual Market. S – Small Group Market. L – Large Group Market. "Form" refers to the language in the insurance contract and typically is required when a new plan is offered in the market (or changes are made to that plan). Rates are filed with the initial form and usually must be filed each time an insurance carrier proposes to change rates for a plan, but the rates are generally not reviewed. "Informational" refers to rate filing requirements where the data is collected and kept by the state, but is not reviewed. "Use and file" means the filing becomes effective when used, though the insurer is required to file rates with the state, which may be reviewed retrospectively. "File and use" refers to requirements where the insurer must file rates with the state, which become effective either immediately or on a date specified in the filing. File and use state may review the rates retrospectively after the effective date. In this case, states usually base their review on claims and financial data submitted by the insurer to examine if the rates were appropriate for the actual claims experience. "Prior approval" refers to requirements where insurers must file rates with the state, and the state has the authority to approve the filing or disapprove it before the effective date. NAIC rate review information is for the 50 states and the District of Columbia.

[a] If insurer does not meet medical loss ratio standards, the rate filing is subjected to prior approval.

[b] Insurers must still provide actuarial certification.

[c] State imposes medical loss ratio requirements.

[d] On May 9, 2010, then and now former New York Governor David A. Paterson signed into law Governor's Program Bill No. 278, which reinstates the New York State Insurance Department's former authority to review and approve health insurance premium increases before they take effect. The law applies to all rate increases taking effect on or after October 1, 2010.

Limits on publicly accessible rate review data make comprehensive uniform comparisons between states elusive. Only 13 states have public Internet access to rate filings or summary statistics on rates.[47] Moreover, there is considerable variation in how states with rate review regulations make their information public. For example, the Maine Bureau of Insurance posts rate filings only for insurers that are called to present their requested increase at a public hearing, whereas the Oregon Insurance Division publicly provides a list of average rate increase requests and approvals by regulated entities and provides access to individual rate filings and approvals.[48]

In terms of approvals of rate increases, there is considerable variation between states. For example, Oregon approved 68.3% of recent requested rate increases, whereas Massachusetts approved only 14.2%.[49] These differences are likely due to both differences in regulatory standards, geographic variation in health insurance markets, health services utilization patterns, and health provider payment rates. The available public information suggests that states approve, adjust, or reject requests for rate increases primarily based on an analysis of cost trends in relation to rate increases approved in prior years, and that the approved rates can be double-digit percentage increases from the previous year.[50] To illustrate, consider the case of Regence Blue Cross Blue Shield of Oregon, which requested an average annual increase of 26.4% for its individual health plans but was approved for a 17.3% increase effective January 1, 2010.[51] Despite medical costs increasing 12.6% from the prior year and a financial loss of 9.7% ($15,476,565) on these policies over the period of May 1, 2008, through April 30, 2009, Oregon decided that the lower rate increase was appropriate because Regence had received an approved average rate increase of 26.5% on the same policies for the previous year.[52] By contrast, Health Net Health Plan of Oregon's individual health plans requested and received a significant average annual rate increase of 22.8% effective on October 1, 2009.[53] Oregon believed that the increase was justified because Health Net lost money on these policies each year between 2005 and 2008 (in aggregate $1,436,505) and it had received average rate increases less than the average increase in medical costs for four of the past five years.[54]

Federal Rate Review under ACA

The Patient Protection and Affordable Care Act (P.L. 111-148, ACA, as amended) includes provisions to increase transparency of proposed rate increases, but it does not go as far as to include a formal approval process for proposed increases. Specifically, the Health and Human Services (HHS) Secretary must, in conjunction with the states, establish a process for the annual review of "unreasonable" increases in rates for health insurance coverage beginning in the 2010 plan year.[55] The term "unreasonable" is not defined by the law and presents a challenge in preventing unintended consequences such as providing additional market leverage to large, national for-profit companies over small, local non-profit insurers.[56] The complexity of making such a determination generally requires analysis of multiple factors by actuaries and accountants. Such a review generally does not lend itself to the use of simplistic benchmarks such as merely prohibiting double-digit percentage rate increases. As the National Association of Insurance Commissioners (NAIC) notes:

> The process should identify "potentially unreasonable" increases, with further review by states and/or the HHS Secretary to determine any mitigating or exacerbating factors and decide whether the increase is actually unreasonable. Any increase that is necessary to avoid a future financial loss on the block of business is usually considered reasonable, unless there are compelling reasons to determine that it is unreasonable. Rates that produce a financial loss can affect consumers by impairing the financial soundness of the insurer, reducing the insurer's incentive to provide good customer service, reducing the insurer's incentive to continue providing coverage and shifting costs to other blocks of business.[57]

Health insurance issuers will be required to submit to the HHS Secretary, and the relevant state, a justification for an unreasonable premium increase prior to implementation of the premium, and the HHS Secretary will publicly disclose the information.[58] The justification requirement does not provide the HHS Secretary with the authority to prohibit the plan from implementing the rate increase. In other words, this is a "sunshine" provision designed to publicly expose premium increases determined to be unreasonable. On December 23, 2010, the HHS Secretary issued a notice of proposed rulemaking for the ACA rate review provisions, with a comment period ending February 22, 2011.[59] The HHS Secretary proposes that when the average increase, alone or in combination with prior increases in the preceding 12-month period, is 10% or more then the rates will be subject to more review to determine if they are unreasonable. The proposed regulation stipulates that HHS would be adopting a state's determination of what an unreasonable rate increase is if the state has an effective rate review program. The proposed regulation specifies that a state's rate review program would be considered effective if the state has the legal authority to obtain the data and documentation necessary to conduct an effective examination. Further, the state must have the ability to review the data and documentation submitted in support of the proposed rate increases, including an examination of the reasonableness of the actuarial assumptions used by the insurer, the validity of historical data underlying the assumptions, and the insurer's accuracy with past projections. If the state does not have an effective rate review program, the Secretary proposes that HHS would conduct the review. HHS would determine that a rate increase is unreasonable if:

- *The rate increase is excessive.* The premium charged would be considered excessive if it is unreasonably high in relation to the benefits provided. HHS would consider if the rate increase results in a projected future loss ratio below the medical loss ratio standard required under Section 2718 of the PHSA. HHS would also consider if any of the assumptions on which the rate increase is based are not supported by evidence or do not support an increase of the magnitude being proposed.
- *The rate increase is unjustified.* Health insurance issuers would be required to provide certain data and documentation to HHS supporting the proposed rate increase. If the data and documentation submitted are incomplete or inadequate then the proposed increase would be determined to be unreasonable.

- *The rate increase is unfairly discriminatory.* A proposed rate increase would be unfairly discriminatory if it results in premium differences within similar risk categories that are not permissible under applicable state law or, if no state law applies, do not reasonably correspond to differences in expected costs.[60]

To support the premium rate review process, ACA requires the HHS Secretary to carry out a program of grants to the states. These grants have an appropriation of $250 million for states to use during the five-year period beginning with FY2010.[61] On August 12, 2010, HHS announced that 42 states and the District of Columbia were awarded $43 million in grants during the first cycle of funding. On February 24, 2011, HHS announced a second cycle of funding of approximately $200 million, for which states will be given multiple opportunities to apply for funds. "On September 20, 2011, HHS awarded $109 million to 28 States and the District of Columbia."[62]

Final Rule on Rate Review

CMS published the final rule implementing the rate review provisions in ACA in the *Federal Register* on May 23, 2011.[63] The final rule clarifies which proposed rate increases would be subject to review (i.e., defining "unreasonable" rate increase), establishes a process for rate review to be conducted either by the state or CMS, and specifies notice requirements to inform the public about the process and outcome of the rate reviews. The final rule also includes a comment period,[64] for which it solicits comments on whether individual and small group health coverage sold through associations should be subject to ACA's rate review requirements.

The final regulations implementing the ACA rate review provisions are not intended as a substitution for existing and future state review of rates. Throughout the final rule, CMS refers to the ongoing authority of states to impose filing requirements and conduct their own review of rates.

Definition of "Unreasonable" Rate Increase

Beginning on or after September 1, 2011, a proposed rate increase will be tentatively considered unreasonable, and therefore subject to review under ACA, if the increase either is 10% or more (over a 12-month period beginning on September 1), or meets or exceeds the state-specific threshold (applicable to a 12-month period beginning on September 1). The 10% threshold is for transitional purposes only, until the state-specific thresholds are established. In developing a state-specific threshold, the HHS Secretary will consult with a state and may review relevant information provided by other stakeholders. The rate review process (described below) will determine whether or not the proposed rate increase is unreasonable, and relevant information about each review conducted will be published online.

Preliminary Justification

For each proposed rate increase subject to review, a health insurance issuer must submit a Preliminary Justification, which is composed of the following:

- Part I—a summary of the proposed rate increase, including claims experience, utilization and cost trend projections, changes in benefits, claims and non-claims costs, current and projected premiums, and a three-year history of rate increases for the insurance product.
- Part II—a justification for the rate increase, including description of data and assumptions used, explanation of primary factors driving rate increase, and description of overall experience of the insurance product, including expenses and loss ratios.
- Part III—a rate filing document. (Instructions regarding the compliance with Part III will be provided through CMS guidance.)

Parts I and II must be submitted to CMS and the applicable state (in a state that already has a mechanism in place to accept rate submissions from issuers). Part III must be submitted to CMS. In addition to the data and documentation components described above, CMS may request additional information if the insurer's submission is insufficient for making a determination. Parts I and II will be posted on the CMS website, with a disclaimer that describes the purpose of the Preliminary Justification. CMS also will provide information through its website regarding the process by which the public may submit comments on the rate reviews that CMS conducts.

Rate Reviews Conducted by State or CMS

Reviews of the proposed rate increases will be conducted either by a state or CMS.

A state will conduct the review if it has an "Effective Rate Review Program" (described below), and it discloses to CMS its analysis for making the determination whether or not a rate increase is actually unreasonable. CMS will accept the state's determination and post the state's decision online. If the rate is determined to be unreasonable and the issuer is allowed under law to implement the proposed increase, CMS will provide the state's determination and explanation to the relevant issuer.

CMS will conduct the review if the state does not have an Effective Rate Review Program. Under this scenario, CMS will apply three tests to determine whether a proposed rate increase is unreasonable or not:

- Is it excessive? Will the proposed increase lead to premiums that are unreasonably high in relation to the benefits provided?
- Is it unjustified? Are the data and documentation provided by an issuer incomplete, insufficient, or otherwise lacking in relevant information that reasonableness of the proposed rate increase may not be determined?
- Is it unfairly discriminatory? Will the proposed rate increase lead to premium differences among insureds that share similar risk profiles that either are not allowed under state law, or do not comport with differences in expected costs?

After completion of each rate review, CMS will post its final determination on its website and provide explanation to the relevant issuer.

As discussed above, a state will conduct the rate review if it has an Effective Rate Review Program. CMS will evaluate (and may re-evaluate) whether a state has such a program in place, according to the following criteria:

- The state collects data and documentation from issuers that are sufficient enough to examine (1) the validity of assumptions used to develop the proposed rate increase, and (2) past projections and actual experience.
- The state conducts effective, timely reviews of such data and documentation.
- The state's review process includes the examinations described above, which takes into account factors specified in the rule that may impact rates (factors such as medical trend, benefit and cost-sharing changes, and others).
- The state's review of rates is based on statutory or regulatory standards.

A state with an Effective Rate Review Program will be required to publish on its website Parts I and II of the Preliminary Justification for proposed rate increases. Moreover, the state must establish a mechanism to receive comments from the public regarding those proposed increases.

CMS reviewed all available state regulatory documentation and met with state insurance regulators to determine if a state had an Effective Rate Review Program. As of July 1, 2011, 40 States, the District of Columbia, and the U.S. Virgin Islands have effective review for all insurance markets and issuers (see table 6).

Table 6. States Determined by CMS to have an Effective Rate Review Program

December 9, 2011

State	Effective Rate Review Program for Individual Market	Effective Rate Review Program for Small Group Market
Alabama	No	No
Alaska	Yes	Yes
Arizona	No	No
Arkansas	Yes	Yes
California	Yes	Yes
Colorado	Yes	Yes
Connecticut	Yes	Yes
Delaware	Yes	Yes
District of Columbia	Yes	Yes
Florida	Yes	Yes
Georgia	Yes	Yes
Hawaii	Yes	Yes
Idaho	Yes	Yes
Illinois	Yes	Yes
Indiana	Yes	Yes
Iowa	Yes	Yes
Kansas	Yes	Yes
Kentucky	Yes	Yes
Louisiana	No	No

State	Effective Rate Review Program for Individual Market	Effective Rate Review Program for Small Group Market
Maine	Yes	Yes
Maryland	Yes	Yes
Massachusetts	Yes	Yes
Michigan	Yes	Yes
Minnesota	Yes	Yes
Mississippi	Yes	Yes
Missouri	No	No
Montana	No	No
Nebraska	Yes	Yes
Nevada	Yes	Yes
New Hampshire	Yes	Yes
New Jersey	Yes	Yes
New Mexico	Yes	Yes
New York	Yes	Yes
North Carolina	Yes	Yes
North Dakota	Yes	Yes
Ohio	Yes	Yes
Oklahoma	Yes	Yes
Oregon	Yes	Yes
Pennsylvania	Yes	No
Rhode Island	Yes	Yes
South Carolina	Yes	Yes
South Dakota	Yes	Yes
Tennessee	Yes	Yes
Texas	Yes	Yes
Utah	Yes	Yes
Vermont	Yes	Yes
Virginia	Yes	No
Washington	Yes	Yes
West Virginia	Yes	Yes
Wisconsin	Yes	Yes

Table 6. (Continued)

State	Effective Rate Review Program for Individual Market	Effective Rate Review Program for Small Group Market
Nebraska	Yes	Yes
Nevada	Yes	Yes
New Hampshire	Yes	Yes
New Jersey	Yes	Yes
New Mexico	Yes	Yes
New York	Yes	Yes
North Carolina	Yes	Yes
North Dakota	Yes	Yes
Ohio	Yes	Yes
Oklahoma	Yes	Yes
Oregon	Yes	Yes
Pennsylvania	Yes	No
Rhode Island	Yes	Yes
South Carolina	Yes	Yes
South Dakota	Yes	Yes
Tennessee	Yes	Yes
Texas	Yes	Yes
Utah	Yes	Yes
Vermont	Yes	Yes
Virginia	Yes	No
Washington	Yes	Yes
West Virginia	Yes	Yes
Wisconsin	Yes	Yes
Wyoming	No	No
American Samoa	No	No
Guam	Yes	Yes
Northern Marianas Islands	No	No
Puerto Rico	Yes	Yes
Virgin Islands	Yes	Yes

Source: Center for Consumer Information & Insurance Oversight, Centers for Medicare and Medicaid Services, "List of Effective Rate Review Programs," December 9, 2011.

Final Justification

Upon receipt of a determination that a proposed rate increase is unreasonable, the health insurance issuer may:

- Decline to implement the proposed increase or choose to implement a smaller increase. The issuer must notify CMS of either action. However, if the smaller rate increase still meets or exceeds the applicable threshold, the issuer must submit a new Preliminary Justification for that smaller proposed increase.

or

- Implement the rate increase that was determined to be unreasonable, if allowed under law. In this case, the issuer must (1) submit Final Justification to CMS (which will be posted on the CMS website for three years), (2) post on the issuer's website: Parts I and II of the Preliminary Justification, the determination and explanation from the rate review conducted by the state or CMS, and the issuer's Final Justification; and (3) make this information available on the issuer's website for at least three years. The Final Justification must be consistent with the Preliminary Justification in terms of the information submitted to justify the rate increase.

CMS Impact Analysis

The final rule includes analysis conducted by CMS on the potential impact of the rule on health insurance issuers and enrollees, rate filings, and administrative costs. Those analyses are summarized below.

Given that the rate review requirements apply to all individual and small group coverage (with the exception of grandfathered health plans),[65] CMS collected and analyzed data on the number of insurance carriers that offer products in those markets, many of which operate in both the individual and small group markets. CMS estimated that 417 issuers potentially would be impacted by the rate review requirements. By market segment, 311 issuers could be affected in the individual market; 342 issuers in the small group market. With respect to enrollees, this would translate to nearly 35 million enrollees potentially affected by rate review (approximately 11 million in the individual market and 24 million in the small group market).

CMS also estimated the number of rate filings that potentially would be subject to review and require justification, and developed low-, middle-, and high-range estimates for both the individual and small group markets.

- For 2011, CMS estimated the number of rate filings in the individual health insurance market that would be subject to review and require the submission of a justification report could range from a low of 279 filings to a high of 819 filings. These estimates represent 40%-67% of all filings in the individual market for 2011.
- For the small group market, CMS estimated a low of 189 filings could be subject to review and require justification, and a high of 940 filings. These estimates represent 20%-32% of all filings in the small group market for 2011.

CMS also estimated the potential administrative costs to issuers related to rate review under ACA. Similar to the analysis on the number of affected rate filings, CMS developed low-, middle-, and high-range estimates of potential administrative costs, based on the 417 issuers estimated to be affected by the rate review requirements (see above).

Table 7. Estimated Administrative Costs to Issuers Related to the Rate Review Provisions in ACA, Year One

	Estimated total cost	Estimated average cost per issuer
Low-Range Assumptions		
One-Time Costs	$10,425,000	$25,000
Ongoing Costs	561,600	1,347
Total Year One Costs	10,986,600	26,347
Mid-Range Estimates		
One-Time Costs	12,510,000	30,000
Ongoing Costs	2,142,800	5,139
Total Year One Costs	14,652,800	35,139
High-Range Estimates		
One-Time Costs	14,595,00	35,000
Ongoing Costs	5,513,600	13,222
Total Year One Costs	20,108,600	48,222

Source: Rate Increase Disclosure and Review, Federal Register, Vol. 76, No. 99, May 23, 2011.

Note: Estimated costs are stated in 2010 dollars. Estimated total cost for all issuers that are responsible for reporting.

Table *7* displays the estimated costs for developing and providing justification reports, retention of records, and online notification requirements (as discussed in the final rule).

APPENDIX. PRIVATE HEALTH INSURANCE COST-SHARING

Other Insurance Costs Not Included in the Premium

Health insurance premiums generally represent only a part of the insured individual's or family's costs incurred under a given benefits plan for health services and prescription drugs. While enrollees and policyholders pay premiums irrespective of health service use, they typically are responsible for cost sharing in the form of deductibles, flat dollar co-payments, and/or percentage co-insurance only when services are used.[66] Increased cost sharing has been viewed by some as a method of shifting costs to those who are utilizing the services, thus limiting the shared risk and constraining premium growth.[67] On the other hand, increasing cost-sharing reduces the value of the coverage at the same time premiums are going up. Essentially individuals and families end up paying more for less, due to exposure to higher out-of-pocket costs.

Similar to the observed increases in premiums, cost-sharing expenses have been increasing.[68] Thus, some individuals may be able to afford purchasing the insurance, but not be able to afford the cost of utilizing health care services despite being insured. From a consumer perspective, deductibles have the most impact because coverage does not start until the enrollee spends more than the deductible amount. As illustrated in *Figure A-1*, average deductibles generally have been increasing the past few years, across plan types in both the group and non-group markets. Comprehensive data on other benefit designs such as drug co-payments and hospital co-insurance are not publicly available. However, the Milliman Medical Index estimates that for a typical family of four with private employer group coverage, out-of-pocket cost sharing has increased between 5.4% and 10.5% annually between 2006 and 2010.[69]

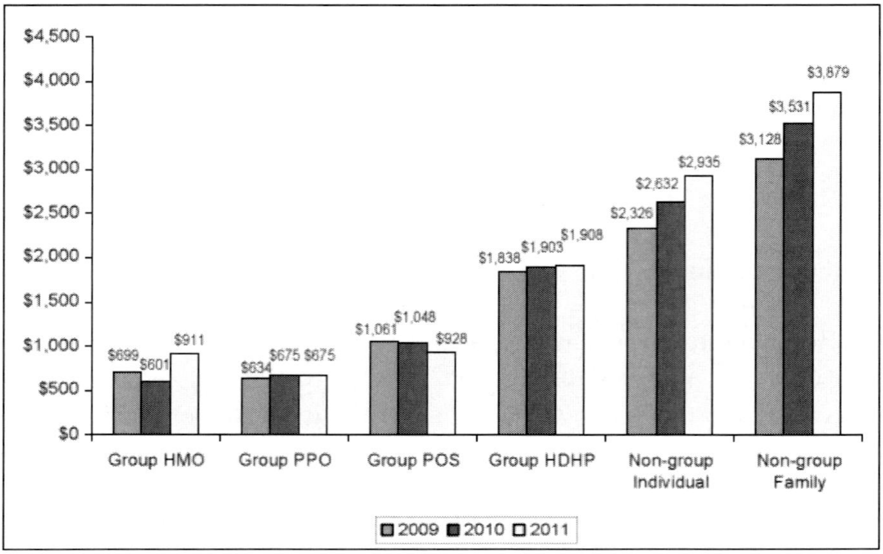

Source: For group health plans, Kaiser/HRET Survey of Employer-Sponsored Health Benefits available at http://ehbs.kff.org/. For non-group health plans, "The Cost and Benefits of Individual and Family Health Insurance Plans," eHealthInsurance.

Notes: HMO means a health maintenance organization. PPO means a preferred provider plan. POS means a point of service plan. HDHP means high deductible health plan.

Figure A-1. Average Deductibles, by Health Insurance Plan Type, 2009-2011.

End Notes

[1] The three private health insurance market segments are individual, small group, and large group. They are defined at §2791(e) of the Public Health Service Act (PHSA). The term "individual market" means health insurance coverage offered to individuals (and potentially their dependents) that is not in connection with a group health plan. The determination of whether an employer is large or small depends on its average employment level for the year. Prior to ACA, the PHSA defined a small group in terms of 2-50 employees, and a large group in terms of 51 or more employees. Section 1304(b) of ACA amended these definitions so that a small employer is one with 1-100 employees and a large employer has 101 or more employees. However, Section 1304(b)(3) of ACA allows states to continue to define an employer with up to 50 employees as a "small employer" until 2016.

[2] The term "insurance product type" refers to substantive differences in plan design (e.g., no deductible versus a high deductible) that would reasonably be expected to affect the utilization of medical care.

[3] For more information on the use of different health insurance rating methodologies, see John Bertko, "Health Insurance Market Rating Practices," September 2008, available at http://www.rand.org/pubs/testimonies/CT315/.

[4] Health insurance actuaries apply mathematical expertise, statistical knowledge, economic and financial analyses, and problem-solving skills to help health insurance companies evaluate ways to manage risk. For more information on actuarial science, see American Academy of Actuaries, "Becoming an actuary," 2010, available at http://www.actuary.org/becoming.asp.

[5] The term "asset risk" means the potential for a default of principal and interest or loss in fair value of assets such as bonds, loans, real estate, and stock. The term "underwriting or insurance risk" refers to the risk that medical expenses will exceed the premiums collected. The term "business risk" refers to the variety of general operational risks to the insurance company such as unexpected increases in labor costs and exposure to litigation. For a general overview of solvency standards, see National Association of Insurance Commissioners, "Risk-Based Capital General Overview," July 2009, available at http://www.naic.org/documents/committees_e_capad_RBCoverview.pdf.

[6] In the case of employer group coverage, the PPI survey takes into account the amount paid by the employer. Yearover-year refers to a comparison of prices to the same time period in the previous year, such as a month or quarter. For example, comparing the percent change in prices in January 2009 to the prices in January 2010. This type of analysis is appropriate for health insurance because coverage typically begins on the first of each month and the duration of the coverage is typically a year.

[7] The most recent exception is this trend is for 2010-2011, when the employer share of the total premium increased slightly.

[8] CRS analysis of data from the Annual Social and Economic (ASEC) supplement to the Current Population Survey (CPS).

[9] Cathy Schoen et al., "State Trends in Premiums and Deductibles, 2003–2010: The Need for Action to Address Rising Costs," The Commonwealth Fund, November 2011.

[10] For example, see Senate Health, Education, Labor and Pensions Committee, "The Affordable Care Act: The Impact of Health Insurance Reform on Health Care Consumers," January 27, 2011; Senate Health, Education, Labor and Pensions Committee, "Health Reform and Health Insurance Premiums: Empowering States to Serve Consumers," August 2, 2011; and House Committee on Small Business, "New Medical Loss Ratios: Increasing Health Care Value or Just Eliminating Jobs?," December 15, 2011.

[11] The health insurance company financial data that could most directly demonstrate specific plan level medical and administrative expenses that drive premiums generally is proprietary and confidential. Regulatory filings such as those with the Securities and Exchange Commission or the state insurance commissioners are reported at the legal entity or parent organization level. In other words, aggregate financial data for an entire company or the company within a state do not reflect the variations in both premiums and costs observed in each of the multiple plans offered by a single organization.

[12] Cost is the product of the price of health benefits and the utilization of those benefits. Profit margin is a financial ratio used to assess the profitability of a firm. It equals revenue minus expenses divided by revenue. Different organizations have different strategic business goals that can also change over time. Maximizing profit may not always be the goal for a given time period. For example, a for-profit company may accept lower profit margins for a period of time in order to gain more market share by offering a better price compared to the firm's competitors. While non-profit insurers do not seek to generate profit in the conventional sense, they have an incentive to reduce expenses in order to invest retained

earnings back into the organization for capital expenditures such as purchasing additional information technology, expanding customer service operations, or other administrative activities.

[13] Rounded to the nearest tenth of a percent. Not all health insurance companies are required to report to NAIC. Most notably self-insured employer groups nationwide and health maintenance organizations in California do not report to the NAIC. National Association of Insurance Commissioners, "Statistical Compilation of Annual Statement Information for Health Insurance Companies in 2010," 2011.

[14] The term "member month" refers to each month of coverage for an enrollee or policyholder; thus a member for a full year would have 12 member months. PMPM calculations are often used for health insurance financial statistics because enrollments and premium payments are generally made on a monthly basis.

[15] The health benefit expenses are nominal amounts (i.e., not adjusted for inflation).

[16] Drug prices generally involve national-level negotiations between pharmacy benefit managers working on behalf of health insurers and drug manufacturers or distributors. By limiting the number of negotiating entities and make the negotiations more national in scope, the geographic variation of prescription drug prices is limited. By contrast, the pricing of health services involves health insurance companies negotiating at the local level with thousands of individual providers, provider groups, agencies, long-term care facilities, and hospitals.

[17] P. Ginsburg, "Wide Variation in Hospital and Physician Payment Rates Evidence of Provider Market Power," November 2010, available at http://www.hschange.com/CONTENT/1162/#ib2.

[18] R. Berenson, P. Ginsburg, and N. Kemper, "Unchecked Provider Clout In California Foreshadows Challenges To Health Reform," Health Affairs, vol. 29, no. 4.

[19] Fallon Community Health Plan v. Division of Insurance, Docket No. R2010-07, August 6, 2010.

[20] Office of Attorney General Martha Coakley, "Investigation of Health Care Cost Trends and Cost Drivers," January 2010.

[21] Congressional Budget Office, "Increasing Transparency in the Pricing of Health Care Services and Pharmaceuticals," June 5, 2008.

[22] Segal Consulting, "2012 Segal Health Plan Cost Trend Survey," September 15, 2011, available at http://www.segalco.com/publications-and-resources/multiemployer-publica tions/sur veys-studies/?id=1733.

[23] U. Reinhardt, "Does The Aging Of The Population Really Drive The Demand For Health Care?" Health Affairs, 2003, vol. 22, no. 6 (hereafter cited as "Aging").

[24] Steven Cohen and William Yu, "The Concentration and Persistence in the Level of Health Expenditures over Time: Estimates for the U.S. Population, 2005–2006," Agency for Healthcare Research and Quality, February 2009.

[25] U.S. Census Bureau, National Population Projections Table 12. Projections of the Population by Age and Sex for the United States: 2010 to 2050, 2008. Available at http://www.census.gov/population/www/projections/summarytables.html.

[26] See B. Strunk, P. Ginsburg, and M. Banker, "The Effect Of Population Aging On Future Hospital Demand," Health Affairs, Web Exclusive, vol. 25, no. 3; and "Aging."

[27] Utilization review includes prospective reviews, often called prior authorization (PA), that attempt to constrain health care costs by reducing unnecessary or inappropriate medical care before the care takes place. For example, a plan might conduct a preadmission review to certify the need for a hospitalization and assign an initial length of stay. Case management includes care coordination and the use of evidence-based medicine to ensure the highest

probability of positive outcomes in a cost effective manner. For example, for a member with heart disease, a plan might coordinate between a primary care physician and a cardiologist to ensure that there is no duplication in services, such as prescribing the same drug twice. Physician gatekeeping means requiring that a plan member get a referral from a primary care physician before being able to see a higher-cost specialist. For more information on utilization management, see T. Wickizer and D. Lessler, "Utilization Management: Issues, Effects, and Future Prospects," Annual Review of Public Health, 2002, vol. 23.

[28] J. Zwanziger and G. Melnick, "Can Managed Care Plans Control Health Care Costs?" Health Affairs, Summer 1996, vol. 15, no. 2.

[29] CRS Report R40834, The Market Structure of the Health Insurance Industry.

[30] Generally speaking, enrollees in PPO and POS plans have more choice of providers in that they can go out-ofnetwork (OON) and pay more cost sharing than they would for an in-network provider. By contract, HMO enrollees generally would have to pay all or substantially all of the cost for OON services.

[31] Kaiser Family Foundation and Health Research Educational Trust, "Employer Health Benefits 2011 Annual Survey," September 2011.

[32] America's Health Insurance Plans, "Individual Health Insurance 2009: A Comprehensive Survey of Premiums, Availability, and Benefits," October 2009.

[33] For example, see Susan M. Schappert and Elizabeth A. Rechtsteiner, "Ambulatory Medical Care Utilization Estimates for 2006," August 2008, available at http://www.cdc.gov/nchs/data/nhsr/nhsr008.pdf; Avalere and the American Hospital Association, "Trends Affecting Hospitals and Health Systems," 2010, available http://www.aha.org/aha/research-and-trends/chartbook/ch3.html; and IMS Health, "Top Therapeutic Classes by U.S. Dispensed Prescriptions," April 2010, available at http://www.imshealth.com/.

[34] Milliman, Inc., "2010 Milliman Medical Index," May 2010, available at http://publications.milliman.com/periodicals/mmi/pdfs/milliman-medical-index-2010.pdf; T. Reuters, "Trends in Spending for Physician Services Among the Privately Insured, 2004 and 2008," April 2010; M. Bundorf, A. Royalty, and L. Baker, "Health Care Cost Growth Among The Privately Insured," Health Affairs, vol. 28, no. 5; and L. Wier, R. Henke, and B. Friedman, "Diagnostic Groups with Rapidly Increasing Costs, by Payer, 2001–2007," June 2010, available at http://www.hcupus.ahrq.gov/reports/statbriefs/sb91.jsp.

[35] Douglas Sherlock, "Administrative Expenses of Health Plans," 2009.

[36] For example, United Health Group is the corporate parent of Golden Rule Insurance Company, which sells several different individual insurance policy products each with their own premium rate calculations. For more information, see Golden Rule Insurance Company, "UnitedHealthOneSM Personal Health Insurance Plans for Individuals and Families," 2010, available at https://www.uhone.com/FileHandler.ashx?FileName=38960LC8-G201008.pdf.

[37] Ingenix itself is a conglomerate that includes the health policy firm the Lewin Group and the actuarial consulting firm Reden & Anders. For more information, see United Health Group "Annual Report for the Fiscal Year Ended December 31, 2009," Form 10-K filing with the Securities and Exchange Commission, available at http://www.unitedhealthgroup.com/invest/2009/UNH-2009-10-K.pdf.

[38] National Association of Insurance Commissioners, "Statistical Compilation of Annual Statement Information for Health Insurance Companies in 2010," 2011.

[39] Net income in 2010 of $2,887,100,000 divided by 2010 membership of 33,300,000 equals $86.70 (rounded) divided by 12 months equals $7.22 (rounded) per member per month.

[40] Wellpoint, 2010 Summary Annual Report," April 2011.

[41] Blue Cross Blue Shield of Rhode Island, "2010 Annual Report," March 2011.

[42] See Alice Rosenblatt, "The Underwriting Cycle: The Rule Of Six," Health Affairs, vol. 23, no. 6; and R. Kipp, J. Cookson, and L. Mattie, "Health Insurance Underwriting Cycle Effect on Health Plan Premiums and Profitability," April 10, 2003.

[43] Investment income refers to income received from investment assets (before taxes) such as bonds, stocks, mutual funds, loans and other investments (less related expenses).

[44] For additional information about state and federal regulation of private health insurance, see CRS Report RL32237, Health Insurance: A Primer.

[45] CRS analysis of state law and regulations from a search of CyberRegs, available at http://www.cyberregs.com/. Also see National Association of Insurance Commissioners, "NAIC Response to Request for Information Regarding Section 2794 of the Public Health Service Act," May 12, 2010 (hereafter cited as "NAIC Response"). For the purposes of this discussion, the District of Columbia is considered a state. Only Missouri, Montana, and Wyoming have no filing requirements for individual and group plans. Three states (Alabama, Georgia, and Mississippi) require filings for informational purposes only. The term "market segment" generally refers to individual, small group, and large group markets. The term "plan type" generally refers to the way health benefits are provided and financed, such as through indemnity insurance or preferred provider organizations.

[46] In any given state, the rate may vary according to the rating factors allowed by the state. For example, rates in the individual market may be prohibited from varying based on health factors, but may be allowed to vary based on age, sex, or other risk factors. The permissible variation in rates establishes theoretical parameters. The actual premiums charged for a set of insurance policies may not span the spectrum of allowed rates; it depends on who applies and accepts coverage.

[47] Those states are CO, CT, FL, IL, ME, NE, NJ, NC, OH, OR, PA, RI, and WI. See "NAIC Response."

[48] Maine Bureau of Insurance, "Filings," May 14, 2010, available at http://www.maine.gov/pfr/insurance/filings/filings.htm; and Oregon Insurance Division, "Summary of Recent Rate Request Decisions," May 11, 2010, available at http://insurance.oregon.gov/insurer/rates_forms/health_rate_filings/rate-request-summary.pdf. The Oregon Health Rate Filings and Public Comments database is available at http://www4.cbs.state.or.us/ex/ins/filing/.

[49] Oregon Insurance Division, "Summary of Recent Rate Request Decisions," May 11, 2010, available at http://insurance.oregon.gov/insurer/rates_forms/health_rate_filings/rate-request-summary.pdf; and Massachusetts Office of Consumer Affairs and Business Regulation, Division of Insurance, "Patrick-Murray Administration's Division of Insurance Announces Decision on Rate Increase Submissions from Health Insurers," April 1, 2010, available at http://www.mass.gov/?pageID=ocapressrelease&L=1&L0=Home&sid=Eoca&b=pressrelease&f= 20100401_hirates&csid=Eoca.

[50] CRS analysis of Colorado Department of Regulatory Agencies, "Annual Report of the Commission of Insurance to the Colorado General Assembly on 2009 Health Insurance," April 1, 2010; Florida Office of Insurance Regulation, "Accident & Health Rate Change Summary 2010 Year to Date," May 03, 2010; North Dakota Insurance Department, "Blue Cross Blue Shield of North Dakota's (BCBS) rate increases requested and approved since 2001," April 9, 2010, available at http://www.nd.gov/ndins/uploads/resources/583/bcbs-chart-web.pdf; Oregon Department of Consumer Business and Services, "Health Insurance in Oregon," January 2010; and Rhode Island Health Insurance Commissioner, "Rate Factor Decisions Announced," March 18, 2010, available at http://www.ohic.ri.gov/2010%20RateFactorReview.php.

[51] Oregon Insurance Division, "Rate Filing Decision Summary Regence BlueCross BlueShield of Oregon Individual Health Insurance," November 13, 2009, available at http://insurance. oregon.gov/insurer/rates_forms/health_rate_filings/health-rate-filing-search. html.

[52] Ibid.

[53] Oregon Insurance Division, "Rate Filing Decision Summary Health Net Health Plan of Oregon, Inc. Individual Health Plans," July 24, 2009, available at http://insurance oregon.gov/insurer/rates_forms/health_rate_filings/healthrate-filing-search.html.

[54] Ibid.

[55] §1003 ACA: §2794(a) Public Health Service Act (PHSA). On April 14, 2010, the HHS Secretary issued a public request for information on the provisions at §2794 PHSA including defining the term "unreasonable," available at http://edocket.access.gpo.gov/ 2010/2010-8600.htm.

[56] Wall Street analysts at Credit Suisse stated that they "believe winners and losers will emerge in managed care. Winners will have access to public-equity capital and invest strategically to offset margin compression by taking market share from 1,200 insurers that may not survive." See Investors' Soapbox PM, "Healthy Picks in Managed Care: Credit Suisse likes UnitedHealth Group, WellPoint, Coventry and Humana," August 17, 2010.

[57] See "NAIC Response."

[58] §1003 ACA: §2794(a)(2) PHSA. Per §2791(b)(2) PHSA, the term "health insurance issuer" means an insurance company, insurance service, or insurance organization (including a health maintenance organization) that is licensed to engage in the business of insurance in a state and that is subject to state law which regulates insurance within the meaning of Section 514(b)(2) of the Employee Retirement Income Security Act of 1974. The term does not include a group health plan, which includes self-insured plans. The term "self insured" refers to group benefits plans (usually sponsored by employers) that take on the insurance risk, rather than contracting with an insurance company to take on the insurance risk (fully insured plans).

[59] 75 FR 81004-81029.

[60] A "risk category" is a classification of a group of insured individuals who share common characteristics, such as age or geographic location, and are covered under a single insurance product.

[61] §1003 ACA: §2794(c) PHSA.

[62] HHS, "Rate Review Works: Early Achievements of Health Insurance Rate Review Grants," September 2011, p. 3, available at http://www.healthcare.gov/law/resources/reports/rate-review09202011a.pdf.

[63] Rate Increase Disclosure and Review, Federal Register, Vol. 76, No. 99, May 23, 2011.

[64] The comment period ended on July 18, 2011.

[65] Grandfathered health plans are group health plans and health insurance coverage (including coverage from the individual health insurance market) in which at least one person was enrolled since the date of ACA's enactment (March 23, 2010). Grandfathered plans are exempt from a majority of ACA's market reforms. For additional information about grandfathered plans, see CRS Report R41166, Grandfathered Health Plans Under the Patient Protection and Affordable Care Act (PPACA).

[66] The term "deductible" means a fixed dollar amount during the benefit period that an insured person pays before the insurer starts to make payments for covered medical services. In other words, there is 100% cost sharing until the deductible amount has been reached. (Though some plans may not apply certain services to the deductible requirement, such as well-child visits, to not discourage the use of such services.) The term "flat dollar co-

payments" means medical cost sharing in a health insurance plan that requires an insured person to pay a fixed dollar amount when a medical service is received. The insurer is responsible for the rest of the reimbursement. The term "percentage co-insurance" means of medical cost sharing in a health insurance plan that requires an insured person to pay a stated percentage of medical expenses after the deductible amount was paid. Thus is the co-insurance is 10% and the medical service is $100 then the member or policyholder would pay $10.

[67] T. Bodenheimer, "High and Rising Health Care Costs. Part 1: Seeking an Explanation," Annals of Internal Medicine, vol. 142, no. 10, 2010.

[68] J. Gabel et al., "Trends in Underinsurance and the Affordability of Employer Coverage, 2004-2007," Health Affairs, Web Exclusive, vol. 28, no. 4.

[69] Milliman Inc., "2010 Milliman Medical Index," May 2010.

INDEX

A

B

C

I

J

L

M

T

U

V

W